D1635703

Applied Theatre: Resettlement

WITHDRAWN FROM
THE LIBRARY

UNIVERSITY OF
WINCHESTER

KA 0420044 6

The **Applied Theatre** series is a major innovation in applied theatre scholarship, bringing together leading international scholars that engage with and advance the field of applied theatre. Each book presents new ways of seeing and critically reflecting on this dynamic and vibrant field. Volumes offer a theoretical framework and introductory survey of the field addressed, combined with a range of case studies illustrating and critically engaging with practice.

Series Editors

Michael Balfour (Griffith University, Australia)
Sheila Preston (University of East London, UK)

Applied Theatre: Aesthetics
Gareth White
ISBN 978-1-4725-1355-7

Applied Theatre: Development
Tim Prentki
ISBN 978-1-4725-0986-4

Applied Theatre: Research
Radical Departures
Peter O'Connor and Michael Anderson
ISBN 978-1-4725-0961-1

Related titles from Bloomsbury Methuen Drama

Performance and Community: Commentary and Case Studies
Edited by Caoimhe McAvinchey
ISBN 978-1-4081-4642-2

Affective Performance and Cognitive Science: Body, Brain and Being
Edited by Nicola Shaughnessy
ISBN 978-1-4081-8577-3

Applied Theatre: Resettlement

Drama, Refugees and Resilience

Michael Balfour, Penny Bundy, Bruce Burton,
Julie Dunn and Nina Woodrow

Series Editors
Michael Balfour and Sheila Preston

Bloomsbury Methuen Drama
An imprint of Bloomsbury Publishing Plc

B L O O M S B U R Y
LONDON · NEW DELHI · NEW YORK · SYDNEY

UNIVERSITY OF WINCHESTER

792 022
BAL   04200446

Bloomsbury Methuen Drama

An imprint of Bloomsbury Publishing Plc

50 Bedford Square
London
WC1B 3DP
UK

1385 Broadway
New York
NY 10018
USA

www.bloomsbury.com

**BLOOMSBURY, METHUEN DRAMA and the Diana logo are trademarks of
Bloomsbury Publishing Plc**

First published 2015

© Michael Balfour, Penny Bundy, Bruce Burton, Julie Dunn, Nina Woodrow, 2015

Michael Balfour, Penny Bundy, Bruce Burton, Julie Dunn and Nina Woodrow
have asserted their right under the Copyright, Designs and Patents Act,
1988, to be identified as authors of this work.

All rights reserved. No part of this publication may be reproduced or
transmitted in any form or by any means, electronic or mechanical,
including photocopying, recording, or any information storage or retrieval
system, without prior permission in writing from the publishers.

No responsibility for loss caused to any individual or organization acting on
or refraining from action as a result of the material in this publication
can be accepted by Bloomsbury or the author.

British Library Cataloguing-in-Publication Data
A catalogue record for this book is available from the British Library.

ISBN: HB: 978-1-4725-2464-5
PB: 978-1-4725-3379-1
ePDF: 978-1-4725-3263-3
ePub: 978-1-4725-2239-9

Library of Congress Cataloging-in-Publication Data
A catalog record for this book is available from the Library of Congress.

Typeset by Deanta Global Publishing Services, Chennai, India
Printed and bound in India

The book is dedicated to all the children and young people we worked with in Logan, Australia.

Contents

List of Illustrations

Acknowledgements

The origins of this book began with a telephone call. Mercedes Sepulveda from MultiLink Community Services in Logan City, Australia had been awarded a small grant to run a short programme aiming to help newly arrived migrant and refugee individuals understand a little bit more about the expectations, issues and services available to them. She thought drama might be a way to do this, and through various conversations, ended up ringing the applied theatre team at Griffith University. Without Mercedes, and without the call, this book would not be. Over the last 7 years through several small and aligned projects we have built up a strong partnership, ultimately leading to an Australian Research Council Linkage grant.

We are indebted to the many MultiLink Community Services staff members and community elders who have worked with us throughout these years. Our special thanks to Shona Doyle whose insights and passion sustained the partnership. Shona has guided us, scolded us (when we got too academic), laughed with us, and has been a strong contributor to the development of the practice. Our deepest respect and admiration to all the community workers, educationalists and elders we have worked with who work tirelessly under considerable stress, anxiety and pressure. The incessant policy changes, competitive funding rounds (pitching community support organizations against each other) and challenges of the sector remind us that the ecological environment is a volatile space to inhabit. We have had first-hand experience of the sensitivity, care and dedication of so many professionals who transcend limited job descriptions to try to make a difference every day.

We'd like to thank all the staff, teachers and administrators in the primary, secondary and TAFE contexts where we worked (who can't be named for ethical reasons). The partnerships that were developed in each context were rich, dialogical and inspiring. We have come away with such deep respect for their dedication, care and imagination.

Our deep gratitude goes to all the participants who were so gracious and willing to play, even if they were, at times, unsuspecting. They forgave us our accidents, our assumptions, and were utterly patient with helping us to understand what was needed and what mattered. We still don't know, but we are getting better at playing and listening a little bit more attentively.

Our thanks also go to Penny Glass and Sarah Woodland who worked as facilitators on the project and to the students from the Bachelor of Arts in Contemporary and Applied Theatre, Griffith University who supported elements of the work. We'd also like to thank Keithia Wilson and Merrilyn Bates who worked with us on the early stages of the research and the late John Stevenson who mentored us through the process of applying for the research grant.

Our final thanks go to Nina Woodrow, who is a co-author, and has been our invaluable research assistant for the last 3 years. She has dragged us into using new research technologies, interviewed, collated and transcribed hours of interviews and workshop notes, shared her extensive experience as a language instructor, co-facilitated workshops, made short films, read and reviewed literature and been a genuine colleague and friend.

Notes on the Authors

Michael Balfour is Chair, Applied Theatre, at Griffith University, Brisbane, Australia. His research expertise is in the social applications of theatre – theatre in communities, social institutions and areas of disadvantage and conflict. He is the recipient of four Australian Research Council-funded projects: Developing Refugee Resilience; The Difficult Return: creating new approaches to arts-based work with returning military personnel and their families; Captive Audiences: the impact of performing arts programmes in Australian prisons; and Playful Engagement and Dementia: understanding the efficacy of applied theatre practices for people with dementia in residential aged-care facilities. Contact: m.balfour@griffith.edu.au

Penny Bundy is an associate professor and member of the Applied Theatre team at Griffith University. One of her key research interests is the impact of engagement in process drama. She has been a chief investigator on several Australian Research Council-funded Linkage Projects, including Moving On, Sustaining Culture, Theatre Space and Developing Refugee Resilience. She was a co-winner of the 2003 American Alliance for Theatre in Education Distinguished Dissertation Award and is co-editor of the Intellect journal, *Applied Theatre Research*. Contact: p.bundy@griffith.edu.au

Professor Bruce Burton PhD is Chair in Applied Theatre at Griffith University, Australia, and is an academic, teacher, playwright and theatre director. He has been the recipient of six Australian Research Council grants in the past 12 years involving the research and development of programmes that have helped students to deal with conflict and bullying in schools, enabled adult survivors of childhood abuse to move on from the trauma they suffered and explored the experiences of young people as theatre audiences as well as the Arrivals research. He is the author

UNIVERSITY OF WINCHESTER
LIBRARY

of eight books in the fields of drama education and applied theatre and has trained a generation of drama teachers in Australia. Internationally, Bruce has been a visiting scholar at Cambridge University in the United Kingdom, and a visiting professor at both Boras University and the Sahlgrenska Institute at Gothenburg University in Sweden. Contact: b.burton@griffith.edu.au

Julie Dunn is an associate professor at Griffith University where she teaches in a range of undergraduate and postgraduate courses across the fields of arts education, applied theatre and educational communication. Her research is focused on improvised and playful forms of drama and the application of these forms within school and community settings. Julie is currently a chief investigator on two major Australian Research Council-funded grants: Playful Engagement and Dementia and Developing Refugee Resilience. Julie has recently taken up the role of editor *of NJ: The Journal of Drama Australia*. Contact: j.dunn@griffith.edu.au

Nina Woodrow has a background in community arts, and a history of involvement in oral history, community theatre and storytelling projects. She has also had a parallel career as an adult literacy and English language teacher in the Australian adult education sector. Working with young people and refugees she has developed arts-based, drama and digital storytelling methodologies as a way of engaging those with stories to tell and language and literacy skills to learn. In 2010 she moved from language teaching to a research position at Griffith University and she commenced a PhD in digital storytelling at Queensland Institute of Technology in 2012. Contact: nina.neptune@gmail.com

Preface

This book is the result of many contributions, experiences and conversations with a range of partners and participants. The final shaping of the book comes from the process of designing and developing three unique case studies of participatory drama and other arts-based approaches involving newly arrived children and young people from refugee backgrounds living in Logan City, Australia. In compiling a book that stories these projects into neat chunks of text, we do not want to give the impression of efficiency. The research process that underpins it has been a messy, creative and absorbing process filled with dialogue, feedback and the testing out of practices in diverse and responsive contexts.

In articulating the distinctive elements of our practice and research we've deliberately tried to address this messiness, by allowing each project team to explore the work of their sub-project in unique ways. What we have tried to do in each case study, however, is to let the research tell its own story – providing readers with an access point into the practice and our journeying process. We have also tried to resist simply reporting back on case studies, sealing these narratives into definitive lessons. Instead, as a research team we feel that after 3 years of research and 6 years of practice in the Logan community, we are still only dimly aware of what is needed to support settlement and how to play and learn effectively in these contexts. That might make us slow learners, but learning slowly with deliberation, reflection and an acknowledgement of this unique community ecology is intended as a mark of respect.

Also embedded within our work is a commitment to reflexivity: an awareness of and explicit understanding of our political, social and cultural position in the research process. This is particularly important in a text such as this one, for the following material clearly reveals that each member of the team was present in the work, not a neutral observer, but a deeply entangled co-learner in the journey.

Finally, in creating this book we are keenly aware that our attempts may conceal and congeal important narratives, and in this context in particular, risk reproducing powerlessness inside the representational scheme of research and practice. How our participants' experiences are described, represented, analysed and reinvented in the meaning-making strategies of our writing is therefore an important ethical concern. As a formal research project we undertook standard ethical procedures of informed consent, feedback and consultation. Wherever possible we involved practitioners and participants in sharing our process and the ideas they generated at various stages. To this end, our main community partner, MultiLink Community Services, has been involved in contributing to and reading over the manuscript to generate dialogue and feedback. Indeed, it is important to acknowledge that this work evolved based on long-term relationships developed over the past 6 years. However, in spite of all of these approaches, we are aware that we may nevertheless have still fallen into some of the traps we hoped to avoid.

The book is structured into seven main chapters, with the first of these being designed to introduce the reader to our project, its aims and approaches, while the next offers an overview of the conceptual landscape of refugee studies, focusing in particular on resilience and resettlement. Chapter 3 offers a framing of the arts and drama practices that were used across the case study projects, while the three chapters that follow offer an in-depth exploration of these practices in action. Rather uniquely, these case studies offer an insight into the life cycle of young people from a refugee background: from the very young to teenagers and unaccompanied adolescents and young adults. In all cases, these children and young people had arrived in Australia within the last 18 months, with some having arrived as recently as a few weeks before their involvement in our projects. From a range of different homelands and each with their own unique arrival stories, what almost all shared was the pressure to succeed, to settle and in doing so provide hope and a passage for others to follow.

In that same spirit, the book concludes with a final chapter that offers a discussion of what we learnt across the three studies. We hope that this material might create an alternative passage for others engaged in refugee work to follow or at least to review. Of course drama does not operate in a vacuum and the social context within which it is delivered is critical. As this book goes to press, Australia is once again in the international spotlight because of its border protection policies and treatment of individuals seeking refuge, including young children. Perhaps this is all the more reason why this book is important, contributing in a small way to the discourse around settlement processes within Australia and beyond. Our experiences across the past 3 years suggest that these young people deserve no less than our fullest attention.

1

Introduction

The main need for individuals who are new arrivals is to feel safe – safety is crucial particularly in the early stages and then having information about what they are going to find in the new space . . . that and supporting them and ensuring that they are not undermined as human beings . . . with people treating them as if they don't know anything . . . but they know things differently. There is an expectation here that because they come from a third world country, that they don't know.

Resilience can be supported by valuing each person, not because he is a refugee, but because he is a person. This is crucial. Here you never take off that label of being a refugee, that you came as a refugee. You know that I have been here 23 years and I'm still a foreigner and you have to prove and prove and prove that you are able to have your own thinking and your own way of surviving. . . . Of course you have opportunities too, but that label of being a refugee is never taken away.

Mercedes Sepulveda, a refugee support worker

If I was the prime minister, I would ask people what their needs are . . . and build from there. If you set up a system without even asking people what their needs are, then you will never succeed. If I was the prime minister, I would change everything . . . I would allow the people to determine their own needs and work through them. I would find out what people can do, not what they can't. But as soon as you arrive, you have someone else determining your needs and the activities you have to do, the language programs you will do. . . . Language classes don't recognize how people learn. I was not happy to be there, I was there because the government told me I had to be.

Biruk: A refugee support worker from the Sudan

The two voices offered above remind us, somewhat painfully, that the settlement journey for an individual with a refugee background can be long and difficult. Confronted by systems that dehumanize and societies that are not always welcoming, the process of establishing a new life is fraught with challenges. Navigating these challenges is potentially more difficult for individuals who have experienced trauma in their homelands, or indeed during their journeys towards a new life. For these people, the obstacles they face in the settlement process can exacerbate their existing anxieties and fears. Disconnected from family networks, the familiarity of cultural practices and established patterns of daily life, individuals like Mercedes and Biruk, can easily feel like their identity has been stripped away from them and that bureaucratic processes are denying their individuality. In such situations, irrespective of their personal resilience, it is the social milieu they enter that can determine how positively they feel about and respond within their personal journey of settlement.

The research described in this book was designed to engage with children and young people undertaking these journeys, specifically those who have relocated to Logan – a rapidly growing Australian regional city bordering Brisbane, the capital of Queensland. Generated in partnership with MultiLink Community Services, a local refugee support agency, and funded by an Australian Research Council Linkage grant, the research extended across a 3-year period (2011–13). Three sub-projects involving participants across a range of age groups and contexts were created. Adopting a qualitative approach that drew upon action research and reflective practice methods, each case study was built upon pilot work developed in these same contexts.

In planning the overarching project, our initial vision was to use drama-based approaches to support settlement, specifically the resilience of individuals. However, as the various projects unfolded, and our understanding of the world of the newly arrived refugee expanded, we quickly became aware not only of the challenges we would face, but indeed of how limited our understanding of refugees, settlement and resilience were.

In many ways then, this book is as much about our team and our journey towards understanding as it is about the young people we worked with. For example, it examines how our understanding of resilience shifted from us seeing it as a personal trait, a quality or set of abilities that can be developed in individuals over time, to a more holistic understanding of resilience as a process, that is context bound, complex and for some, fragile. An individual or indeed a community's resilience is to a great extent determined by the specific social context within which they are operating at any given moment.

Similarly, our understanding of the challenges of settlement and our capacity to make a positive contribution also shifted. Two earlier projects had given us some insights into these challenges, while a number of meetings with MultiLink team members soon revealed others. These challenges ranged from successfully navigating driver's licence testing procedures through to more complex and significant processes such as dealing with child custody and child protection agencies. Unfortunately, in spite of persistent and dedicated attempts by our team to work directly with the government agencies responsible for these processes, in effect to support resettlement by working from our own side of the cultural fence, it soon became clear that there was significant resistance within some government agencies to our involvement, especially through the application of dramatic approaches. Like the newly arrived individuals and families we were hoping to support, it seemed that we were speaking a different language, that our 'knowing' was different and that these differences excluded us.

Fortunately, we found a more welcoming response from local educational institutions, especially those with an existing and highly positive relationship with MultiLink. The partnerships that eventually developed were with a local primary school, a large secondary school and a Technical and Further Education (TAFE) College. With a different focus, approach and set of team members working in each of these contexts, the three projects developed their own settlement goals and outcomes. What they shared, however, was an emphasis on the development of English language skills. This emphasis was not predetermined, but rather emerged as we engaged with the various institutions. All shared the belief that language development is a critical part of the settlement process and there was general acceptance across these institutions of the positive role that participatory forms of drama might play in this area.

We began slowly however, searching for the most appropriate forms of drama and the most effective ways of engaging with each group of newly arrived young people. For example, in the primary school case study, our first instinct was to draw on our skills as facilitators of process drama for we were aware of and convinced by the growing body of literature that has recently been reported in the area of process drama for additional language learning.[1] However, we were somewhat hesitant about how well this particular dramatic form might work with beginner language users with no shared language and whose literacy development in their first language was minimal or non-existent. We could find no evidence of anyone having tried process drama in such contexts before and therefore wondered if an alternative approach might be needed. For this reason, the primary school pilot study was a critical component of our approach.

We also began slowly in the secondary and TAFE projects, creating different cycles of action and data collection, being responsive to the needs and confidence of the young people we worked with. This slow approach enabled us to tread carefully, trying out ideas, listening and observing, and enacting new cycles and applying new approaches as our participants showed they were ready for them.

Our data-collection processes were also diverse and built up over time, with each project gently including the collection of photographs, artworks, observations, artefacts, video recordings of sessions and finally, interviews. This diversity of sources was aimed at creating rich and 'thick' textures to sift through and offered the possibility of assessing multiple layers of data.

---

[1] This literature will be outlined and discussed in Chapter 3.

Clearly then, the initial stages of our work involved identification of appropriate sites, consideration of the particular needs of the individuals within those sites and selection of drama and other arts-based approaches that might be most suitable in these contexts and for these purposes. Of course, we also needed to consider how we would deal with the personal stories of our participants, and in relation to this aspect of the work we recognized that we had three options – engaging with these stories directly, avoiding them entirely in favour of symbolic or fictional material, or finally, focusing only on personal stories that related to post-arrival experiences.

In considering these options, we were keenly aware of the fact that within the context of arts-based work, especially theatre, personal testimony is often seen as a key means of empowering newly arrived individuals through the sharing of subaltern experience with a wider audience. However, as Jeffers (2008) warns, these stories can also be interpreted as problematic representations of victimhood. Preoccupied with personal narratives and particularly drawing on the traumatic past, these theatrical representations can be conditioned by the judicial context within which stories are constructed. Indeed, the very category of refugee performance can create an essentialist frame from which the extrication of practice is almost impossible. The effort to construct a discourse about refugee performance is therefore enmeshed in an unwavering paradox. Put simply, how may practice deal with refugee stories when the stories themselves (bureaucratic performance, personal stories as victimhood, suffering as spectacle) make an encounter with alterity more elusive?

We were also mindful of the age of the children and young people we would be working with and our limited expertise in supporting trauma victims, and therefore determined that the most appropriate approach would be to avoid, where possible, the use of pre-arrival stories. Instead, we decided that a more effective approach would be to make use of stories and materials that would offer an appropriate level of distancing and emotional protection through symbol and metaphor. However, in line with our exploration of settlement processes, we agreed that it would be appropriate for some groups and individuals to share personal narratives relating to experiences post arrival.

The social ecology of the local context – Logan City

As part of the consultative process for this project and its three case studies, it was important for us to understand the social ecology of the local area we worked within, including how, where and why individuals with a refugee background sought help and support. The notion of community and social ecology draws from the Aristotelian concept of eudaimonia (often translated as flourishing), the process of understanding aspects of life when considered as a whole. Importantly then, members of the research team had worked in the Logan area since 2007 and had developed a number of important local partners and interested multi-disciplinary collaborators. It is important to underline that both in terms of logistics and in relation to the quality of the dialogue between the practice and research, long-term partnerships are critical in navigating the complexities of issues at play within any given community. The most important of these relationships was of course with MultiLink Community Services, an organization begun in 1989 primarily to provide support and English classes to newly arrived refugees and migrants. The organization has grown now to offer services across the lifespan and has become a community-based organization that works with other grass roots organizations in the area and within a tight budget to address the local political and social issues faced by diverse individuals and their communities that call Logan home.

First settled by Europeans in the early 1800s, Logan City is now a rapidly growing regional city (Logan City Council). It first came to the attention of the governor of New South Wales when Captain Patrick Logan wrote a letter to say he had discovered a river south of Brisbane and expressed the notion that it was a place worthy of the attention of settlers. Since then, the Logan region has become an area that settlers and migrants from all over the world have flocked to. Over the years, world events have changed the demographics of the people arriving in the area and Logan is now a city which can claim to be home to over 215 different ethnic, religious and cultural groups, with all evidence pointing to this increasing. Logan boasts 26 per cent of its population being born overseas (Logan City Council).

One of the unique features of Logan as an area, however, is that despite its ethnic diversity of Samoan, Aboriginal, new migrants and humanitarian entrants, it has resisted ethnic enclaves. There are no specific areas, streets or suburbs defined or designated for or by specific ethnic or cultural groups. As such, its neighbourhoods are often a rich mix of ethnicities from many different countries.

Most refugees and asylum seekers who eventually settle in Logan City come from refugee camps or marginalized areas in urban settings, where the most basic resources and services were scarce or inappropriate to good health. Many of these individuals and families have experienced difficult events, such as prolonged periods of deprivation, loss of identity and culture, human-rights abuses and the loss of family members. Hence a significant proportion of the newly arrived in Logan are likely to have multiple and complex health problems on their arrival. Shona Doyle, a programme manager with MultiLink, observes:

> Upon resettlement, refugees or humanitarian entrants carry the burden of their past, which can include war, persecution or family loss. When this is coupled with the resettlement process, often in low socio-economic areas, where all is unfamiliar, living on a budget that initially seems to be a lot of money and having to acquire another language, the resettlement process can be overwhelming for someone who has already had to endure so much change in their lives. We can see that once the physical and safety requirements of the individual are relatively satisfied and achieved through what is often described as the honeymoon period, people face problems ranging from culture

shock and PTSD, to food insecurities and health and well-being issues including the management of chronic disease. In addition, most struggle to have their needs of belonging and building of esteem met.

Informing projects in Logan City

In October 2007, members of the research team were invited by MultiLink to develop a theatre project with newly arrived humanitarian entrants from Burundi and Ethiopia living in Logan City. The Department of Immigration and Citizenship (DIAC) funded the project that aimed to use the arts to disseminate experiences about Australia's culture. Its steering group, made up of representatives from Burundi and Ethiopia, signalled that there were significant settlement problems within their community groups. With each group of new arrivals similar difficulties emerged, ranging from pragmatic domestic issues (learning to cook with a gas cooker, understanding how to use an ATM, etc.) to the more complex negotiation of understanding new cultural paradigms and values. The community representatives suggested that beyond the initial 'honeymoon' period of arrival, individuals and groups encountered considerable stress and anxiety in dealing with the acculturation process. Askland (2005), drawing on Giddens' (1991) work, supports this view and found that many newly arrived young people from Timor living in Australia suffered from a loss of ontological security, a loss that undermines their sense of control, trust and power. Within school and community settings, this lack of security and identity led to adjustment issues including delinquent behaviour, attention problems, aggression or withdrawal (Allwood et al. 2002).

In response to the concerns outlined by MultiLink, it was determined that a Forum Theatre approach would be adopted that would use community stories of settlement to share with newly arrived groups. Forum theatre is a participatory drama form originally developed by Augusto Boal (1979) that was initially used to support individuals to overcome oppression. Here, actors create scenes based on stories shared by a number of individuals. In this way, the stories become fictionalized, allowing them to be safely used to promote discussion of the issues represented within them.

The first stage therefore was to gather stories and experiences from Burundian and Ethiopian community members who had been residents for 4–5 years, complemented with interviews with community elders/ leaders, and other community organizations. There was a deliberate request for a broad range of stories, not just issue-based experiences but funny, surprising and unusual observations about living in Australia. The collated material from these responses provided a rich resource of anecdotes, reflections and moving accounts of settlement difficulties. We then worked with a team of community actors drawn from a range of ethnic backgrounds who volunteered for the project. The actors included a single mother from Ethiopia (her 1-year-old son played a cameo) and three other actors. The stories highlighted the considerable pragmatism and resilience needed in the process of making and unmaking 'home'. As one of the participants in the project defined it:

> Here is where I am living, because I came from that home, where I call home. I've seen there's no home there. There's nothing, completely nothing. So, I am still alive and I've found somewhere to call home. Now I am at home, where I am living in peace. I am doing everything, so it's home for me. (personal notes 2008)

The performance that resulted from these interviews was made up of several scenes. The first started with a dream and the excitement of arrival. This was followed by the mother's growing frustration in finding work because of her lack of English and transferable qualifications. The second focused on the father of the family and was based on community concerns about the high incidence of domestic violence and child abuse among refugee families. It showed how this fictional father was dealing with the dramatic change in his status within the family and socially. The third scene focused on one of the daughters – and highlighted a common issue in which the younger generation pick up English faster and become more adept at negotiating a new culture. The relative speed of adaption and, in particular, the 'rights' that they see other Australian children having exist in tension with more traditional family values.

The structure of the performance of these three scenes was simple. A MultiLink presenter (translated by an interpreter) introduced the play and the invited audience was offered a brief outline and background to the fictional family and a plot summary for each scene. The language employed in the scenes was basic, with ideas being shown rather than spoken. Each scene ended in a dilemma, a problem not resolved within the drama, on which the audience is invited to comment. In the presentation, the action was stopped after each scene. The facilitator checked with the audience to see whether the story had been clear and then asked for suggestions from the audience to help advise the characters about what they could do.

The performance was rudimentary; it had a 'job to do' and reflected the need to communicate experiences clearly using basic language. The show was performed for three different audiences, with diverse responses. The Burundian audience responded with a high level of enthusiasm, demanding the actors come onstage to explain themselves (in character). In classic Boalian style, advice, scorn and observations flowed with ease. The second performance was to a group of Afghani women who had asked to see the play. Culturally they provided a very different response. The women were generally quiet when asked for questions or comments, but there was considerable whispered debate between them. The third audience group responded with a heated discussion between young and old community members engaged in a rich discussion (conducted in four languages) about the merits of 'traditional values'.

The MultiLink facilitator encouraged these debates, and also referred the audience to support networks. In this way, the specific needs of the audience were identified through the focus of the discussion. Following the performance a large feast was prepared for audience members. The discussions flowed, with considerable enthusiasm, continuing out of the theatre space and into the eating space.

The audience responses and questions recognized the extent of the difficulties of acculturation. For example, one woman in the audience explained that the concept of social security or any form of government support was impossible for her to understand. Another response related to the difficulties of budgeting and managing money after a long period in a camp. Another significant issue for the audiences was that of landlords, who after the first 6 months (in which rents are paid directly to them via social security) terminate contracts, leaving individuals and families to move at short notice. The intergenerational issue also attracted considerable response. The discussion in the Ethiopian group reflected on how, in newly arrived families, the older children are offered places in schools, and both English and cultural awareness develops more quickly for them than for the adults. The mother and father (if they are both in the country) feel more isolated by having to look after younger children and/or being unemployed and therefore have little opportunity to gain confidence in the language and culture.

Despite the limited scale of the project, the nature and richness of the stories from the process highlighted important issues. The stories aimed to enable a peer group of performers to communicate experiences of settlement to an audience of new humanitarian arrivals. The focus was on offering opportunities for the discussion of the problems that might occur, and the pragmatic support strategies that might be available. The project deliberately eschewed 'public' performance in favour of an invited and specifically targeted audience. In this way, the audience governed the content of the event. It led to a focus on survival strategies and tactics of resilience, with attention to the pragmatic present and the possibilities of the future. The practice stemmed from a strong analysis of the needs of new humanitarian groups, as articulated by community organizations, community representatives and the volunteer performers. The project emphasized 'ownership' of the material and the stories were constantly aligned to the priorities of the community, in terms of what community members felt was important to represent. The narratives were generalized fiction, based on personal accounts, but rendered universal by the process. Emphasis was placed not on who was telling the story (or whose story it was) but on the pragmatic 'what' of the story, in terms of offering strategies to deal with specific issues. The aesthetics were straightforward and functional, although perhaps a little neglected in the rush to encompass all the other objectives of the project. Certainly there was no 'cultural specificity' in the style and the form, and this was perhaps its greatest weakness.

A number of other projects flowed from this initial partnership, including an interactive performance (Woodland and Lachowicz 2013) aimed at helping new migrants with understanding Australian history and the requirements of the Australian citizenship test, and Living Stories, a community project working with refugee actors that toured to local schools.

As a result of these projects we had built up a strong level of engagement with partners and participants across the Logan region. We felt that we were starting to understand and feel more a part of the local community and were therefore more confident as we made the decision to explore avenues for further collaboration. In the section below, an introduction to the three case studies that emerged as a result of these collaborations will be outlined.

The case studies evolve

As noted above, the three case studies at the heart of this book were integrated into educational contexts, with each one having its own unique agendas and interdependencies. Accordingly, each project had its own goals and purposes, while the nature of the integration within the broader educational institutions changed and shifted over the life of each case study cycle. For example, in the secondary school case study, an explicit issue relating to how newly arrived teenagers in the language unit were integrated into the wider school community was identified. There, despite a culturally diverse student body, issues of bullying and intimidation had emerged. This situation therefore became the starting point for the team, eventually leading to the development of a peer education process that sought to support, not only the newly arrived students but their peers from non-refugee backgrounds.

By contrast, the primary school project developed solely in response to a call for more diverse and engaging approaches to the teaching of English. Situated within a special education unit offering intensive language learning for newly arrived 5–12-year-olds, this project emerged through a partnership with the school principal and his staff.

Finally, the TAFE project, involving unaccompanied minors and newly arrived young adults, attempted to explore language engagement through a multi-arts approach, with the goal of enhancing language acquisition, social awareness and confidence.

In each context then, there was a need to negotiate, listen and consider how best to work alongside our partner professionals in a way that would lead to a flourishing of practice rather than a resistance or resentment of practice. In the primary school, for example, the principal, like almost all contemporary school leaders, was under pressure to maximize school-wide results within national benchmark testing, specifically the National Assessment Program – Literacy and Numeracy (NAPLAN) tests. Despite its multi-cultural population (and high rate of newly arrived students), the academic performance of all students, irrespective of their arrival status, is used to generate statistics that are then benchmarked against those of other schools that do not have the same ethnic diversity. Similarly, in the TAFE context, extensive paper work was required to demonstrate the extent of language learning for all students in every class.

From the perspective of our partner professionals then, the danger of drama-based approaches can be that they are seen as a diversion and a threat to the very real bureaucratic pressures individuals are under. The more we understood these pressures, the more we were able to work with teachers and institutions to support their objectives and programmes. The key here was respect for the work of the professionals that work within these communities day in and day out, who were there before us and will be there after us. Understanding the community ecology and our place within it was simply a mark of respect and consideration. Also understanding too how we could work within and with the ecology was important. There was a strong desire for new and inventive ways of working with students and the young people, and from our perspective we welcomed the implicit and explicit knowledge that the educational professionals shared with us. The relationships were dialogical and evolved and deepened over the span of the research.

Before moving on in later chapters to describe the work completed within the three case studies and discuss the outcomes generated by them, we now offer an introductory examination of the notions of refugee and resilience, positioning our philosophies in relation to them.

Who is a refugee?

The question of who is a refugee has been posed and argued about by scholars, policymakers and agencies since well before the Convention on the Status of Refugees came into force on 22 April 1954. That convention defines a refugee thus:

> A person who, owing to a well-founded fear of being persecuted for reasons of race, religion, nationality, membership of a particular social group or political opinion, is outside the country of his nationality and is unable or, owing to such fear, is unwilling to avail himself of the protection of that country; or who, not having a nationality and being outside the country of his former habitual residence as a result of such events, is unable or, owing to such fear, is unwilling to return to it. (UNHCR 1979)

While the chaos following World War II was one of the drivers for developing the convention, one of the events also contributed to the momentum happened in the build-up to the war. This event took place on 13 May 1939, when the German liner MS *St Louis* sailed from

Hamburg, Germany, to Havana, Cuba. The ship carried 938 passengers – the mass majority of whom were Jews fleeing from the Third Reich from Germany and Eastern Europe. Even before the ship sailed, it was uncertain if the passengers would be allowed to disembark in Cuba before seeking visas for the United States.

The resentment and political manipulation of the ship's impending arrival was subject to considerable media and public debate. The MS *St Louis* became a symbol of partisanship. Large anti-Semitic rallies were held in Cuba, denouncing the influx of refugees who, it was felt, would take up precious jobs and resources. Eventually Cuba accepted 28 passengers, but the remainder sailed for Miami in the hope of direct pleas to US authorities:

> Sailing so close to Florida that they could see the lights of Miami, some passengers on the *St. Louis* cabled President Franklin D. Roosevelt asking for refuge. Roosevelt never responded. The State Department and the White House had decided not to take extraordinary measures to permit the refugees to enter the United States. A State Department telegram sent to a passenger stated that the passengers must 'await their turns on the waiting list and qualify for and obtain immigration visas before they may be admissible into the United States'. (United States Holocaust Memorial Museum 2013)

Following the US government's action to deny entry, the MS *St Louis* sailed back to Europe where some were able to secure entry visas to Great Britain, Netherlands, Belgium and France. A total of 533 passengers were trapped by the advance of the Third Reich in Western Europe and of those 254 died during the Holocaust.

This story has generated considerable attention because it vividly illustrates the hopes and dilemmas facing refugee groups, and the way their stories become warped by political machinations, popular resentment and test our collective will and associated guilt. The pervasive image of boat people in need of sanctuary is a powerful and divisive one, no more so in contemporary Australia and other 'developed' nations. The example of the MS *St Louis* highlights how societies often fear the other and seek to repulse ethnic groups fleeing a war because it seems to threaten a way of life, or take up resources, or because of a fear of foreign unknowns undermining the national identity by infiltrating the body politic dramatically and irreconcilably. The fact that the MS *St Louis* episode, viewed with the hindsight of history, is recalled by the US and Canadian authorities as shameful and marked by apologies and memorials does not help. Instead, the fear and panic of boat people continues to galvanize radical opposition and bitter polemics that sees even the most committed left-wing parties participating in a race to the bottom to securitize borders and pander to fear and popularism.

The refugee issue is therefore more than just another political agenda. It is an issue that galvanizes public discourse and policy into a metonymic refugee crisis. In Western cultures, national security and ethnic identity have become entwined in the political and public imagination. Few other issues create such a deep-seated emotional and often irrational debate that fuels and frustrates even the most committed commentator, practitioner or policymaker. As Faulkner (2003, p. 95) notes, terms like refugees and asylum seeker function as a 'code word for a range of meanings, variously referring to people as illegal immigrants, scroungers or potential criminals'. Fuelling this perspective, British Conservative politician Michael Howard's speech declares that 'Firm border controls are essential if we are to limit migration, fight crime and protect Britain from terrorism' (Carteris-Black in Jeffers 2012, p. 26). Given such rhetoric, it is not surprising then that the asylum seeker in public discourse is often the distrusted enemy within, the terrorist seeking refuge, the individual bent on being a destabilizing force and taking away resources from existing citizens and communities.

The legal, financial and political ramifications of defining the term refugee in particular ways mean then that the semantics of every word are weighed and carefully scrutinized, especially by State governments. As such, the UN Convention is a useful and in some ways remarkably progressive statement. It points to the violent act of separation that an individual or group goes through when leaving their 'home' State, and identifies the forces that shift them into a period of transition, into a state of legal limbo or liminality. This betwixt and between state is one that is simultaneously legal, psychological, social and economic.

The label of refugee also brings with it a moral status of dependency, with large numbers of stateless individuals and groups being at the mercy of international relief agencies and the benevolence of, often, indifferent (or hostile) neighbouring countries. Only a tiny fraction of those displaced by armed conflict get the option of re-locating to a Western country for repatriation, but as Mercedes's comments at the start of this chapter describe and Rizvi's research suggests: 'Once an individual, a human being, becomes a refugee, it is as though he has become a member of another race, some subhuman group' (Rizvi quoted in Dunbar-Ortiz and Harrell-Bond 1987, p. 232). In spite of the fact that one is not necessarily born a refugee, as Alex Rotus (2004) observes, it is a status bureaucratically designated. It is also culturally and socially defined: 'the refugee exists, by definition, within the community to which he or she does not properly belong . . . they are strangers that we have to deal with, living in a liminal zone amongst and yet not-quite-amongst-us' (p. 54). According to Rotus, the term 'smoothes over differences within the group it designates at the same time as reifying the boundary that defines its otherness and the notions that constitute that boundary . . . notions of displacement and other' (p. 52).

Arts workers, like other practitioners, are caught in the contentious 'crises' discourse surrounding the issue. Working with individuals with a refugee background is as controversial as working in a prison context, and can either inspire curiosity or disdain in equal measure. The rhetoric of unwelcome queue jumper gets mixed up with people with official humanitarian status. It's no wonder that newly arrived individuals, as part of a formal approval process, want to slip the term as quickly and inconspicuously as possible. It is a way of extricating themselves from the jumble of unsettling popular sentiments. The sooner a refugee becomes a new citizen the better.

Set against this backdrop, we have opted within this text (wherever possible from a semantics perspective) to refer to the young people we worked with as 'being from a refugee background' or as new arrivals, rather than as 'refugees'. We hope that in adopting this terminology we are able to avoid otherizing the children and young people who participated so willingly and enthusiastically in the three projects. We also hope that this approach serves, in a small way, to shift the types of discourses that perpetuate Mercedes's view that the 'label of being a refugee is never taken away'.

Resilience

A growing body of publications across a range of fields has, within the last decade, aimed to illuminate the nature and meaning of resilience (see Chapter 2). Within these, there has been a growing acknowledgement of how social, cultural and economic forces can impact upon resilience. For example, within the beginning teacher literature, a large Australian study has argued 'individualized views of resilience lead to a diminution of the influence of situational and structural forces on human experience' (Johnson and Down 2013, p. 704). These authors go on to argue that the consequences of such views can be serious, for they shift responsibility for human well-being away from the state to the individual and as such, promote simplistic and apolitical conceptions of resilience.

Similarly, within the refugee studies literature, there has been a growing awareness of the role of community, with greater effort being expended to identify the contextual and social factors that support individual resilience. For example, Marlowe's (2010) qualitative study examined the experiences of 24 Sudanese men recently resettled in Australia, with findings suggesting that the picture of resilience painted by the biomedical model that is based almost entirely on individual's trauma stories is dangerously incomplete:

> From an exclusive trauma-focused understanding, a thin description of the individual is created where other important considerations of identity and history (social, political, cultural) are easily lost or hidden.

Thus, the story of a person's experience(s) of trauma associated with forced migration and how it has negatively influenced his/her life can overshadow other co-existing stories which can emphasize something very different about what a person values and readily identifies with. (Marlowe 2010, p. 183)

The study gained an insider's perspective into what helped these men through hardship that included: 'their culture, parental teachings, spirituality and how they maintained hope'. In these cases, Marlowe argues (2010, pp. 195–6), the source of resilience can be seen to reside outside the trauma story, located in culture, history, values, stories and traditions, along with dreams and aspirations for the future.

A study along similar lines in the United States (Goodman 2004) used a narrative approach to examine how 14 recently resettled, young, unaccompanied males from Sudan coped with trauma and hardship in their lives. Four themes were identified in their narratives reflecting the coping strategies they used (Goodman 2004, p. 1177). These were

- collectivity and the communal self
- suppression and distraction
- making meaning
- emerging from hopelessness to hope.

In discussing these themes, Goodman (2004) examines them in relation to the concept of resilience and stresses the importance of recognizing the sociocultural specificity of them. For example, connection to others is central and, 'the social value of representing one's family further facilitated a will to survive' (p. 1192).

Also noted in Goodman's (2004) study was how coping strategies need to evolve over time and the importance of respecting each individual's timetable for healing. In this respect, 'suppression provided a fairly effective means of coping for the refugee youths and should be considered to continue to be an important pattern of coping among this population until other patterns have been developed' (p. 1192). The creative process of meaning making was identified as a critical coping strategy, one understudied in the literature. These boys, 'crafted narratives of hope despite the realities of their daily lives' and 'found meaning in their cultural and religious beliefs regarding suffering and life' (p. 1193). In-depth narrative-based studies such as these help to refocus attention on the idea that in being open to the experiences of refugees negotiating resettlement, resilience is something that may be revealed rather than developed through interaction with helpers.

It is this pre-existing capacity for optimism and resilience that a recent Australian study (Correa-Velez et al. 2010, p. 1406) recognizes. It examined the psychosocial factors associated with well-being outcomes among a cohort of 97 youths with refugee backgrounds during their first 3 years in Melbourne, Australia. According to this study these young people demonstrated a 'high potential for making a good and successful life in Australia', noting that their capacity for optimism and resilience in the first 3 years post settlement was 'powerfully shaped by the prevailing social climate and structures that are openly inclusive or that exclude (Correa-Velez et al. 2010, p. 1406).

Finally, in considering notions of resilience, our team also reflected on the fact that at least some of the individuals we worked with may have already been far more resilient than others already living within the community, and hence our initial desire to develop their resilience may have been somewhat misplaced. This view is informed by the work of Papadopoulos (2007) who has argued that if we view people from refugee backgrounds as universally and permanently depleted by their traumatic histories, then we may be missing something important, underestimating their potential for transformative renewal:

> It is well known that following a difficult and intense experience, people may respond in ways that emphasize the renewing rather than the injurious effects of the experience. Despite (or even because of) the pain, disorientation, disruption, devastation and loss, people may still feel that the very same 'traumatic' experience also made them re-evaluate their priorities in life, change their life-styles and acquire new values – all in all, experiencing a substantial change and renewal

in their lives. Having come so close to death or having experienced the unbearable anguish of substantial losses, people often emerge transformed, reviewing life, themselves and their relationships. This means that, paradoxically, despite their negative nature, devastating experiences (regardless of the degree of their harshness and destructive impact) may also help people reshuffle their lives and imbue them with new meaning. (p. 304)

In the following chapter, further literature relating to the complex and contested concepts at the heart of these three studies is examined.

Part One

2

Refugee Resettlement: Arriving, Becoming, Belonging

Migrant kids are like rivers
Always moving
but somehow still enough to be given a name
like Wog, Nip, Fake – hyphen – Australian
So of course when we learnt to drive
We'd ride for hours in the only place where we felt like we
belonged
somewhere between points A   and B
between the green and the red
I learned to love the traffic lights when they turned amber
because I realized our teachers also slowed down on their
approach to us
and tapped their feet impatiently for our answers

. . .

I am not a hyphen
      I am a 100-metre dash
between my history
and your make believe
b   etween White-Australia policies
and being saved by the colony
      between having to drag my past, kicking, back into my present
and hide it behind my back
                  in your presence. . . .
            Extract from Amber Lights by Luka Lesson (2013).

This rap verse comes from a Brisbane-based poet, Luka Lesson. In the rap he highlights the anger and frustration of the in-between dynamic of being a migrant and/or new arrival. Lesson uses the metaphor of the amber light to draw attention to how 'migrant kids' have to live betwixt one culture and another, never quite inhabiting either space, but taking up residency in an uncertain territory that is neither red nor green.

For those whose lives have not involved the need for migration, settlement sounds like a conflict-free and gentle process, conjuring up images of sediment that gradually comes to rest on the bottom of a slow-moving river. However, for those directly involved in this process, the waters can be turbulent and individuals can be swept along in eddies and currents that make the task of settlement extremely difficult. In addition, for many who have been settled, there is a sense of temporality, a possibility that there will be further changes and indeed that the resettlement process is never ending. Transience is permanent.

For this reason, the chapter's title does not refer to arriving, becoming and belonging as a linear process, but rather, through exploration of the research literature within the field of refugee studies and beyond, attempts to understand more about these emotional qualities as ephemeral, dynamic and perpetually in flux. They inhabit the amber country and are often felt simultaneously in their absence and presence.

The literature includes an extensive body of work that explores the impact on individuals of their pre-arrival experiences, including key work relating to post-traumatic stress disorder and the various approaches that have been applied in an effort to support individuals who are experiencing it. We start here and examine how this predominantly biomedical model and its accompanying literature have shaped much of the research into the repercussions of forced migration as a result of political violence and persecution. In many of these studies we will note that there has been a tendency to ascribe a pathological diagnosis based on defined criteria, running the risk of characterizing groups and their experiences in homogenous ways. We then move on to explore the literature that widens this focus to consider not only the experiences and qualities that individuals bring to the settlement process, but also, and importantly, the responses of those communities where individuals will eventually establish new lives.

Along the way, notions of resilience, settlement and refuge are explored. As such, the chapter points to some of the gaps and silences in the practical and theoretical approaches that have been applied in attempting to understand refugee settlement, and consequently, the way contemporary thinking has been shaped and circumscribed by it. In addition, it outlines some of the policies and procedures that have been used for assisting new arrivals.

Meanwhile, the scale of the global refugee situation is extraordinary and growing. The number of people forcibly uprooted by conflict and persecution worldwide exceeded 42.5 million at the end of 2011. This total includes 16 million refugees and asylum seekers and 26.4 million internally displaced persons uprooted within their own countries, and almost half of all forcibly displaced persons globally are children – over 12 million girls and boys. During 2011, a total of 79,800 refugees were admitted for resettlement in 22 different countries, with 92 per cent of opportunities for permanent resettlement being offered by United States, Canada and Australia (United Nations High Commissioner for refugees [UNHCR] 2011). Since then, the problem has accelerated rapidly.

In response, the refugee studies field has struggled with the task of developing an organizing framework to describe and study refugee resettlement, adaptation and acculturation processes. So far there is little consensus as the debate spans several epistemological and methodological standpoints. As Gifford et al. (2007) note, there is a tension between meaning and measure at the centre of the study of refugee resettlement. They explain thus:

> While qualitative studies of the refugee experience provide valuable insights into the meanings of transition and resettlement, it is difficult to generalize these findings to the broader resettled population. And when it comes to measurement, there are at present very few quantitative instruments that possess the validity and rigor required to assess constructs of psychosocial well-being, health, resilience, and

UNIVERSITY OF MANCHESTER
LIBRARY

other key variables that are associated with resettlement outcomes. (Gifford et al. 2007, p. 416)

The predominance of positivistic/quantitative approaches within the psychology of acculturation and the pervasive use of instruments such as checklists and questionnaires has, not surprisingly, drawn some criticism in recent years. Deficiencies in research methods have created gaps, silences and cultural blindness in the understanding of refugee experiences. These gaps include the fact that few longitudinal studies that focus on change over time (Murray et al. 2010) or mixed-methods approaches have been used (Gifford et al. 2007).

The scope of the conceptual models, theories and approaches that inform the field of refugee studies, and the tensions between various positions adopted within them, speak to the emergent nature of our understanding of the refugee experience. These controversies serve to illustrate the complexity inherent in this field of research, the diversity of thinking that relates to it and the need to remain open to knowledge emerging from multi-disciplinary orientations.

A focus on the individual and the impact of trauma on settlement

Trauma and post-traumatic stress disorder (PTSD) are the most commonly used descriptors for refugee health and well-being. It is understood that experiences such as war, torture and other human rights violations, threats to life, traumatic losses, dispossession and eviction, the experiences of flight, refugee camps and final resettlement in a third country will expose individuals to significant, multiple stressors and result in individuals demonstrating higher levels of psychological disturbance than the general population. While there has been extensive documentation of psychopathology among resettled refugee groups, there are enormous variations in the rates reported. The reported rates of PTSD range from 7 per cent to 86 per cent according to some estimates (Fawzi et al. 1997). An overview of recent studies illustrates this diversity, and also points to a lack of consensus on what evidence there is to support the idea that mental health problems in diverse refugee populations conform to a characteristic pattern of causation and manifestation over time.

A systematic review of the prevalence of post-traumatic stress disorder, major depression or psychotic illnesses in general refugee populations in Western countries was undertaken by Fazel et al. (2005). In this study,

> 20 eligible surveys provided results for 6743 adult refugees from seven countries, with substantial variation in assessment and sampling methods. In the larger studies, 9% ... were diagnosed with post-traumatic stress disorder and 5% ... with major depression, with evidence of much psychiatric comorbidity. Five surveys of 260 refugee children from three countries yielded a prevalence of 11% ... for post-traumatic stress disorder. Larger and more rigorous surveys reported lower prevalence rates than did studies with less optimum designs, but heterogeneity persisted even in findings from the larger studies. (p. 1309)

From these findings it can be interpreted that 'refugees resettled in western countries could be about ten times more likely to have post-traumatic stress disorder than age-matched general populations in those countries' (Fazel et al. 2005, p.1309). Further, the results of this meta-analysis suggest that about 1 in 20 has major depression, and about 1 in 25 has a generalized anxiety disorder.

Using a more nuanced approach, Silove et al. (2007) conducted a study over an 11-year period to identify the significance of PTSD within a large group of new arrivals living in Sydney. They found a 'dose-response association between exposure to pre-migration trauma and risk of mental disorders, PTSD in particular. They concluded that trauma and PTSD continue to affect the mental health of individuals even after a decade or more of resettlement' (p. 469).

In a US project, Tran et al. (2007) collected data from a community-based survey of 349 adult Vietnamese respondents living in an East

Coast metropolitan area. This study found that depression symptoms in resettlement follow an inverted-U pattern where symptoms increase initially and then gradually decrease over time. This study found that it takes approximately 12.5 years for depression levels to decrease. The study concluded that individuals 'suffer from higher levels of psychological problems during their first decade of resettlement' and that it takes 'more than a decade for a non-English speaking immigrant or refugee to adjust psychologically into his/her host society'. (Tran et al. 2007, p. 87).

Quite different findings, however, are reported elsewhere. Beiser (2009), in a decade-long study of 1,348 people newly arrived to Canada from Southeast Asia, found an unexpectedly low risk of psychopathology during the early years of resettlement. The suggested explanation for this pattern is 'the constructive use of suppression to get on with life in the short and medium term' (Beiser 2009, p. 556). Beiser (2009) goes on to describe how opinion is sharply divided on whether psychological intervention in the immediate aftermath of trauma for resettling individuals mitigates distress or conversely impedes recovery from the effects. This research calls into question the assumption that debriefing is critical, and recall of traumatic events should always be encouraged suggesting that

> in the immediate or medium-term aftermath of catastrophe, it may prove most effective to support individual attempts to suppress the past and focus on the present and future. Health care providers should, however, be vigilant about the possibility that years, or even decades after refugees have resettled and apparently effected a satisfactory adjustment, mental health risk based on past experience may resurface, and that resurfacing may be tied to significant adult developmental periods. Context probably affects mental health risk. Failure to achieve occupational success and to establish and maintain an enduring relationship increase mental health risk. Conversely, the presence of these critical factors in an individual's life may provide a supportive context for mental health intervention. (p. 557)

The inconsistencies in reported rates of mental health disorders and patterns of distress have been attributed to the use of different research methods and measures, different diagnostic tools and cut-offs, the use of culturally blind assessment instruments and research designs, variations across refugee cohorts, variations in pre-migration stress and trauma, historical, geographical and political impacts on refugee experiences and so on. What is apparent from looking at this research in general, however, is that efforts to chart transitional patterns of adjustment and to predict the likely rates and timing of mental health disorders can provide only a partial and potentially misleading picture.

For these reasons, survey-based approaches to research on refugee mental health, and indeed the construct of PTSD itself, have been criticized as problematic. Porter (2007) traces these arguments back to Engel (1977), who argued that 'the application of western psychiatric constructs to refugee populations are all examples of a biomedical bias in which disease is internal to an individual and recognizable by deviation from western norms' (quoted by Porter 2007, p. 419). Alternative or complementary research approaches and paradigms that move beyond the biomedical model highlight culturally embedded, political and ecological perspectives to understand the refugee experience. Researchers such as Porter have concluded that pre-migration trauma is only one of the many intersecting factors to be considered when assessing refugee well-being. Porter's (2007) meta-analysis of five decades of worldwide empirical literature on refugee mental health yielded the following finding:

> War and forced displacement are initially social phenomena. They trigger a cascade of direct and indirect effects in a recursive network running within and among social, psychological and biological domains. Refugees experience and respond to a wide range of sequelae, beyond those that are narrowly post-traumatic. Individual effects studied in isolation cannot capture the totality of the refugee experience, which is a changing pattern of activation (both external conditions and internal reactions) within a biopsychosocial framework. . . . A wide range of social variables beyond the acute stressors associated with the

pre-flight and flight periods exert important effects on refugee mental health. These include distal social variables (such as status of source conflict) as well as proximal social variables (chiefly ongoing difficult post-displacement conditions such as limited economic opportunity, poor living conditions, displacement nearer to the source conflict, less permanent residency status in the host country). Furthermore, social variables can interact to create more complex patterns of moderating effects on mental health. (pp. 428–9)

These studies begin to focus on refugee resettlement, and the causal links with notions of resilience and well-being, as manifold and multidimensional – in other words, complex, contingent and messy. Porter (2007), in advocating the usefulness of a multi-disciplinary 'bio-psychosocial' framework, argues that 'interrelationships between the biological, psychological and social domains of refugee adaptation are empirically demonstrable . . . but the social domain is regrettably understudied in the mental health/adaptation literature' (pp. 428–9). In this respect, Silove's (1999) conceptual framework has gained credibility as it unpacks and extends the PTSD model in response to the specific experiences of refugees, providing a structure to allow the interplay between five psychosocial systems – security, attachment, justice, identity and existential coherence – to become visible. The model highlights the value of studying the impact of trauma on a range of adaptive capacities and their analysis points to a bias:

> One such system, the 'safety' system, and its relationship to post traumatic stress disorder (PTSD), has tended to attract much of the focus of recent research, with relatively less attention being given to the impact of trauma on other adaptive systems such as the capacity to form and nurture interpersonal bonds, to retain a sense of identity and role functioning, to maintain faith in a system of justice, and to sustain a sense of existential meaning, coherence, and hope. (p. 200)

In other words, individuals may need support to re-establish the ability to develop personal and community relationships, and develop a renewed sense of identity, purpose and meaning, and these adaptive systems are located in the social domain. The importance of the social domain is also stressed by Australian qualitative researchers Peisker and Tilbury (2003) who reason that the social and cultural capital that can be mobilized in support of newcomers, together with the overall climate created by Australia's resettlement policy and services, is a critical factor in the degree of distress experienced. The shift in perspective offered here is that the host society's general responses to new arrivals are critical elements in their well-being and that the idea of trauma in general

> should be extended to encompass not only the war trauma, but also the 'limbo' period spent in the countries of first asylum (often in refugee camps), where refugees may have depleted their emotional coping resources, as well as post-arrival trauma comprising the language barrier, social isolation, unemployment, poverty, insecure housing, acculturation stress, and discrimination. (p. 82)

Peisker and Tilbury's (2003) study allows a consideration of the impact of the biomedical approach, arguing that the tendency among resettlement services to medicalize the refugee experience may induce new arrivals to adopt a passive and dependent approach to the process of resettling. Their study included two research projects conducted in Western Australia, involving individuals from the former Yugoslavia and the Horn of Africa. The themes discovered, through interviews, participant observations and focus groups, and their subsequent analysis of the effects of the medical versus social inclusion perspectives on refugee resettlement, led to the articulation of a 'four-element typology of refugee resettlement styles'. This typology was arrived at through a process 'akin to the grounded theory approach' and can be summarized as 'predominantly active (achievers and consumers) or passive (endurers and victims)'. The 'passive' profile is described in this way:

> Passive resettlers often perceive their pre-migration experiences of loss of family members, property, and social status as irreparable. Many are greatly concerned about their families back home. Some have spent years waiting for the possibility of resuming a 'normal life', either in war-torn

areas, or in a 'country of first asylum', under temporary protection, (which has been described as) 'the spiritual midway to nowhere'. In the process, their emotional resources and coping ability may have been seriously depleted. Refugee helpers in our sample confirmed the detrimental effects of the extended temporary existence, during which many people were not allowed to work and thus forced into passivity. They live in relative social isolation from mainstream society as well as from their 'ethnic community', reliant on small networks of family and friends for emotional and practical support. (pp. 72–3)

Locus of control is also an issue addressed in Gozdziak's (2004) study analysing the tenets of Western training programmes for helping professions in the refugee field. The observation here is this:

When suffering is defined as a medical problem, it is removed from a public realm and is no longer within the purview or power of ordinary people; rather it is raised to a plane where only professionals – medical or mental health care providers – can analyze and discuss it. Moreover, when refugees suffer as a result of political dissidence or generalized political violence, medicalizing their experiences removes the matter from the political and social context that produced their anguish and loss. (p. 206)

In this way, medicalizing human suffering can be seen to short circuit an integrated, active and community-based response to trauma. Alternative perspectives may instead provide an understanding of how host societies perform in providing a safe, supportive, empowering and culturally inclusive environment and how this may impact on the mental health outcomes for new settlers from refugee backgrounds.

Social acculturation

A psychosocial approach is an alternative way to investigate what conditions best support the well-being of those recently resettled.

The approach here is to focus on the social conditions created by the host society and the communication patterns of individuals and communities as they move through the dynamic process of negotiating resettlement in a particular environment. Berry and colleagues (Berry et al. 2006; Berry and Sam 1997; Berry 2009) formulated a hugely influential framework for acculturation orientation. This model, along with its conceptual frameworks for understanding identity, acculturation and intercultural relations, has become a point of reference for much of the subsequent research and debate in North America, Europe and Australia. Essentially, Berry pioneered the notion that acculturating individuals can orient themselves to their traditional culture, the wider society, to both or to neither. He categorized four acculturation orientations – Integration, Assimilation, Separation and Marginalization. These orientations describe the relative priority migrants place on maintaining their original cultural heritage compared with the importance they place on engaging in intercultural contact with members of the dominant culture. Bicultural integration is viewed as the preferred identified style by most acculturation experts and is associated with the most adaptive outcomes (Rudmin 2010). More recently, however, arguments have been made that acculturation attitudes and orientations are obscured by these 'Berry Boxes'. As Ward (2008) explains:

> The emergence of acculturation strategies obviously occurs as a process and is set in a broader socio cultural context, yet it has most often been examined as a static outcome in itself or as a predictor of broader adaptation. The process elements have been largely overlooked. . . . Berry's model presents us with an orderly framework. . . . But it is not clear how people arrive at these orientations, and if they change over time. . . . Consequently, we believe that it is useful to examine the construct of identity conflict in acculturating individuals and groups. (p. 107)

Ager and Strang's (2008) conceptual framework, while not answering this call specifically, was designed to unpack some of these elements.

The study began with the notion that since integration was frequently seen as a key policy objective, then identification of elements central to perceptions of what constitutes successful integration was a useful starting point. The key domains of integration proposed by these authors related to four overall themes: achievement and access across the sectors of employment, housing, education and health; assumptions and practice regarding citizenship and rights; processes of social connection within and between groups within the community; and structural barriers to such connection related to language, culture and the local environment (p. 166).

A framework linking these domains was then presented as a tool to foster debate and definition regarding normative conceptions of integration in resettlement settings. Important in this framework is the conceptualization of distinct forms of social engagement – 'social connections' (generating social capital) and 'social bonds' (generating bonding capital within a family or one's own ethnic group) and 'social bridges' (generating bridging capital with the wider community and the state). These forms of capital are seen as 'facilitators, understood as removing "barriers" to integration (and) social connection'. These facilitators are seen to play 'a fundamental role in driving the process of integration at a local level. Indeed, local respondents commonly identified social connection to be for them the defining feature of an integrated community' (Ager and Strang 2008, p. 177).

While highlighting the dynamism and interactive factors at play, this model neglects a culturally embodied view of integration. In response, Sonderegger and Barret (2004) conducted a study in Australia that examined culture-specific differences and developmental pathways of acculturative stress among newly arrived young people. Using a comprehensive assessment package of subscales and measures of cultural adjustment, ethnic identity, social support, self-esteem, anxiety and trauma symptom checklists, several hundred primary and high school students located in Southeast Queensland and Melbourne from former Yugoslavia and Chinese cultural groups, who had been living in Australia for different lengths of time, were surveyed.

The data gathered in this study indicated that 'child and adolescent cultural groups have unique cultural adjustment profiles, specific strengths and differentiated needs' (p. 354). As expected, high school students reported higher levels of self-esteem the longer they had been residing in Australia. Some unexpected findings, however, included cultural and gender differences and counter patterns in terms of hopefulness for the future. Primary school students were found to become more optimistic over time but this was not the case for the high school students in the study, who reported experiencing an increasing sense of hopelessness. Adolescent females reported higher levels of pessimism than their male counterparts. The patterns of adjustment also varied along the lines of cultural background.

In essence what can be drawn from the diversity of perspectives and findings represented in this body of research is that while constructs such as acculturation patterns/styles and PTSD have been supported by a substantial amount of empirical evidence, there remains tensions, gaps and silences in the study of refugee resettlement that remain understudied and undertheorized. There is a growing call for further investigations that embrace 'ethnography, participant observations, qualitative interviewing and many other methods of data collection that seem to be crucial for understanding the experience of migrants' (Chirkov 2009).

These kinds of small-scale, in-depth studies, while producing findings that are not necessarily generalizable, can open up new areas of knowledge and indicate a potentially powerful direction for future research. Research that prioritizes the subjective perspectives of refugees themselves and that treats the resettlement process as dynamic, complex and transformative can lead to a deeper appreciation of the phenomenon itself. As Rudmin (2010) advocates: 'A way forward from the field's historically habituated paradigms may be found by returning to the phenomena and looking anew, if possible, at the experience of migration' (p. 308).

As such, there is now a growing body of qualitative studies that aim to understand the settlement journeys of individuals, and based on the stories emerging from these, the concept of 'Adversity-Activated development' theorized by Papadopoulos (2007) is gaining weight in the field. The observation here is that there are individuals who have survived and have even become strengthened by the traumatic experiences of their lives. This perspective is in stark contrast with those that position new arrivals as universally and permanently depleted by their traumatic histories, suggesting that the research to date may be missing something important, underestimating the potential for transformative renewal.

In response to this potential gap, Murray et al. (2010) surveyed the empirical research relating to mental health interventions in resettlement contexts around the world. This study resulted in a call for more personal interventions that recognize the fact that individuals respond in different ways and that these differences are at least partially determined by the social context they are now living within. Their final assessment was that positive outcomes might be best achieved

> by engaging individual clients, families, and whole communities in programs that place emphasis on individual and social growth and change in response to adversity. Programs that give due acknowledgment to community leaders and indigenous wisdom, help build community capacity, ensure cultural salience and significance, and work to minimize power differentials between health professionals and local healing and support systems are more likely to facilitate what Papadopoulos (2007) has labeled adversity-activated development. (p. 582)

This list of suggestions indicates that the pathway to successful resettlement is significantly influenced by the social environment that newcomers encounter, the capacity of the host environment to be welcoming and inclusive and the quality of the experiences young people are exposed to post-migration. Similar factors have also been identified by Correa-Velez et al. (2010, p. 1406) who suggest the following:

> The factors that best predict well-being over the first three years of settlement are those that can be understood to promote a sense of

belonging, becoming at home, being able to flourish and become part of the new host society. . . . Successful resettlement . . . will be determined by the extent to which they are able to become a valued citizen within their new country. The opportunity to flourish, to become at home, to belong is powerfully shaped by the prevailing social climate and structures that are openly inclusive or that exclude.

An ecological view of settlement and resilience

Set against this backdrop, Bronfenbrenner's classical model of child development (1979) has been taken up by several of those writing about resilience and resettlement, particularly for children impacted by armed conflict (Harney 2007; Waller 2001). This model defines a framework for considering the relationships impacting on children and their development. These relationships include those in the immediate settings of school or home (microsystems), those in an extended social network (mesosystems), those within formal and informal society structures such as governments and neighbourhoods (exosystems) and those that extend to the cultural, historical and political sphere (macrosystems). This framework helps to extend perceptions of resilience beyond that of an individual trait and allows us to build a richer understanding of the location and development of resilience in relation to a complex ecological system.

Garbarino and Bruyere (2013) argue that an ecological view of resilience in children and youth who are effected by armed conflict is critical, since a capacity to heal and thrive after traumatic experiences is contingent and dependent on a range of variables in a young person's life. They argue that this focus on context

is the core principle of an ecological perspective on human development and it is essential in developing an understanding of resilience in children and youth affected by and involved in war. It is essential to understand that resilience operates in context, in the sense that it functions within what Bronfenbrenner termed the organismic,

micro-, meso-, exo-, and macro-systems of human experience. This
means it can arise from features of temperament and individual intelligence, relationships with parents and teachers, the degree to which
the various contexts of a child's life provide positive synergy, the degree
to which policy makers outside the child's immediate social experience
make decisions that are child-focused, and the nature of the broader
culture with respect to nurturing, healing, and protecting. (p. 263)

Betancourt and Kahn (2008) similarly argue that 'trauma, psychological adjustment, resilience, and the mental health of children in war
must be viewed as a dynamic process, rather than a personal trait'
(p. 2). The authors of this study recommend the promotion of strategies such as participatory education programmes that 'aim to extend
and enrich social networks might provide young people with important
resources to help them weather the distress associated with war and
displacement' (p. 10).

A study conducted by Ungar et al. (2007) also notes a shift in focus
in Western conceptualizations of resilience, away from a view that
looks for this quality as an individual characteristic to a more ecological
interpretation of resilience. Learning more about culturally determined
indicators of resilience is critical in this view since resilience in this
context depends on the 'capacity of the environment to provide access
to health enhancing resources in culturally relevant ways' (p. 288). To
this end, an international, mixed-methods study of resilience among
youth aged 12–23 was conducted in 14 sites in 11 countries (Ungar
et al. 2007). The qualitative findings from interviews with 89 youths are
reported revealing the way these young people resolved, in culturally
specific ways, the tensions inherent in resettlement. Seven tensions were
identified including 'access to material resources, relationships, identity,
cohesion, power and control, social justice, and cultural adherence'
(Ungar et al., p. 295). Overall, the findings from this study reveal that

youth who experience themselves as resilient, and are seen by their
communities as resilient, are those that successfully navigate their way
through these tensions. Resilient youth find a way to resolve all seven

tensions simultaneously according to the strengths and resources available to the youth individually, within their family, community, and culture. It is the fit between the solutions youth try, and how well their solutions address the challenges posed by each tension, within the social and political constraints of their community, that contributes to a young person's experience of resilience. The data reveal no evidence that one way of resolving these tensions is better than another. There is no causality or linearity, meaning that each youth or adult whose words were captured during the study spoke of the unique ways they succeeded in overcoming adversity. (Ungar et al. 2007, p. 294)

Recently, however, a new angle on the concept of resilience has emerged. This perspective is grounded specifically in work with young people from refugee backgrounds and calls into question the very existence of resilience. For example, Barber and Doty (2013) have argued that if you look at the application of resilience as a concept to the research as a whole on how children and young people adapt and recover from exposure to political violence, then the basic tenets of the resilience construct may be challenged. The authors explain that while the construct of resilience is inconsistently defined in the field of social science, an essential feature of the way it functions is that resilient youth demonstrate an uncommon imperviousness to lasting damage and/or that they somehow have an unusual ability to recover quickly from traumatic experiences. Given this understanding, a paradox is then presented since: 'instead of confirming the viability of the construct of resilience (by revealing that only a limited set of individuals survive the adversities of war), the literature challenges it (showing that most adapt effectively)' (Barber and Doty 2013, p. 237). Thus, a dissonance is revealed:

Ironically, rather than providing the expected clarity as to resilience and its prevalence, examination of the literatures on conflict youth (sic) raises fundamental challenges to the utility of the construct itself. In short, the consensus conclusion from reviews of the literatures is that majorities of youth exposed to or involved in political conflict do not manifest notable dysfunction. This finding appears to directly contradict the expectation from much of the writing on resilience, namely, that only a small minority of youths would be able to function well in such severe contexts. (p. 233)

The discordance arises from the assertion that resilient functioning is 'qualitatively different than positive functioning, development, or coping' (p. 245). While the authors make a point of noting that war exposes children and young people to a context presenting extreme adversity and risk, on the whole refugee youth appear to adapt and reconstruct their lives in a way that refutes the logic of the resilience framework. The perspective is not a suggestion that the true horrors of war be underplayed, and the authors here support the view held by Betancourt and Khan (2008, p. 9) that researchers should not be 'seduced by the optimism of resilience and miss the undeniable, often long term mental health consequences of wartime exposure on child mental health'. However, '"political conflict as a context" for resilience research has received less research attention to it . . . (as compared to other contexts such as poverty, health emergencies, and grief)' (Barber and Doty 2013, p. 236). An important implication of this research is the realization that the way children and young people survive war may actually be viewed as a challenge to the resilience construct, an invitation to develop alternative or more holistic appreciations of this normative human capacity to move forward when injured through the refugee experience.

Lenette et al. (2012), in an ethnographic study among newly arrived, single women in Australia, similarly emphasize the everydayness of the women's achievement of resilience, which speaks both to the diverse pathways these women trod and to the constructivist nature of the way they engaged with the challenges presented in their everyday lives. This study highlighted 'the ordinary nature of resilience in everyday routines, the dynamic processes underpinning the achievement of resilience each and every day over time'. The authors here argue that 'the everyday is not simply a vessel in which lives are lived, rather it is the milieu in which the social processes of resilience are enacted daily' (p. 639). Moreover, the authors suggest that the construction of resilience as extraordinary or exemplary might also

> feed the neoliberal exchange now rooted in refugee policy in many resettlement countries (since) resilience theory can be readily incorporated into neoliberal policy agendas, with its capacity to emphasize the individual over the social, particularly the enterprising resilient citizens who free themselves from dependence on state-sponsored support. (p. 649)

Theories about resilient functioning then are exposed in this resettlement context to a degree that warrants a fresh eye. Claims about the location and temporal manifestation of resilience, about who has and doesn't have resilience, may resonate with an impulse to reinforce mainstream notions of normality through the process of constructing 'the other'. Positioning the individual whose story of trauma and recovery conforms or diverges from the norm of the good new citizen diverts our focus away from the quietly creative process that those in the studies above have demonstrated – of how a fragile resilience is generated, as an act of ingenuity and survival, moment by moment with the resources that are at hand.

Conclusion

In developing the three case studies within this overall project, the literature outlined above has been significant in shaping and informing our practice, not just at the initial design stage, but throughout the process when issues were encountered or when a deeper understanding of resettlement was needed. Although much of it is contradictory and contested, drawing upon a range of organizing frameworks to describe and study resettlement, several important themes nevertheless emerged to guide us. These include the need to be concerned with and recognize the importance of the mobilization of social and cultural capital within communities of new arrivals (Ungar et al. 2007; Peisker and Tilbury 2003), the host society in providing culturally appropriate health-enhancing resources (Ungar et al. 2007; Correa-Velez et al. 2010), being open to culturally embodied views of settlement (Ward 2010; Sonderegger and Barret 2004; Murray et al. 2010), ecological views of resilience and working to engage whole communities in programmes that emphasize personal growth (Murray 2010; Betancourst 2008; Ungar 2007), the role of agency and individual's potential for transformative renewal (Papadopoulous 2007), opportunities that enhance the capacity for individuals to connect with others (Silove 1999; Ager and Strang 2008; Goodman 2008), processes that support identity negotiations (Silove 1999; Ward 2008; McPherson 2010; Collie et al. 2010; Goodman 2004), enhancing the capacity of new arrivals to generate hope and make meaning out of their experiences in culturally relevant ways (Marlowe 2010; Silove 1999; Peisker and Tilbury 2003; Goodman 2004; Khawaja et al. 2008), addressing ethical concerns by creating spaces for individuals to control the agenda of research projects (Ellis and Kia-Keating 2007; Mitchell et al. 2006) and being alert to the way new arrivals are constructing their own personal, culturally meaningful, creative solutions to the particular circumstances that confront them every day – solutions that can be at odds with normative notions of resilience. Instead, this kind of resilience is unfixed, evolving and fragile (Barber and Doty 2013; Lenette et al. 2012).

We hope that in the chapters that follow, our work might contribute to this list by offering different starting points and positions. The case studies that developed were as much a product of local epistemologies (the teachers, community workers and elders, the participants with whom we worked) as the academic and policy discourse on resettlement. The case studies demonstrate and try to illustrate the ways in which different forms of knowledge were interwoven, applied and explored. As the refugee literature acknowledges, the concept of knowledge is complex and contingent. The amber light is always on.

3

Framing the Practice

There has been a recent and growing interest in creating arts-based practice with, by and for refugees and asylum seekers in Western cultures. Or perhaps it is more accurate to say that there has been greater attention paid to documenting and discussing the arts and their role in this area (see Balfour 2013; Jeffers 2012; Thompson et al. 2009). The practice includes projects that facilitate refugee writing, music and performance, dance, theatre and performance, films and the creation of refugee festivals that celebrate diverse ethnicities. Arts-related activities also exist in a number of related contexts, in refugee camps and in third country sites. Some of the work features the active participation of individuals from a refugee background; others use testimonies and stories from new arrivals that are then performed by actors. At the heart of many of these projects is an underlying intention to represent and promote refugee stories as a way to actively circumvent the more aggressive discourses that circulate in many Western cultures about the refugee issue.

However, Burvill (2008) warns against complacency in how the arts represent the refugee 'other'. Arts practices that seek to represent the other may be driven by ethical outrage, but risk over simplification and presenting individuals as either traumatized or oppressed. As Pupavac (2008) notes, the danger is that the performance of refugees is underscored by endearing romanticism and ignores the complex issues of integration and the impact of migration on local communities. As Jeffers rightly provokes, arts projects can sometimes create 'the need for the "right" kind of refugee story in which complexities are smoothed out to create a simple narrative of individual crisis and flight' (Jeffers 2012, p. 46). Despite these caveats many projects are created to construct positive counter-narratives against dominant anti-refugee and asylum-seeker agendas and sentiments. The projects are important efforts in providing balance, empathy and understanding in audiences and the wider refugee discourse. Burvill's (2008) analyses of several productions focused on the stories of refugees and asylum seekers in Australia posit a way through the paradox of representing the other in purely endearing ways. Drawing on Levinas he suggests that performance can interact with audiences to create events that construct an interactive co-presence, one that is a 'constative proposition' rather than a sealed narrative (p. 245).

> For Levinas, we are always already 'hostage' to the other, for whom we have an infinite and therefore 'unassumable' responsibility, which we must nevertheless strive to assume. . . . Certain strategies of narrativisation may tend to provide an audience with a sense of secure knowing, which is less 'productive' of the affect that is essential to the Levinasian ethical encounter. In Levinasian terms, comprehension or knowing about a human situation can militate against openness and response-ability. Perhaps the Levinasian encounter can only occur fleetingly, in powerfully affecting moments. (p. 245)

There have been a number of participatory arts programmes designed to offer individuals with a refugee background opportunities to assign meaning to traumatic experiences, to develop a sense of agency and to assume some control over decision-making (Dennis 2008; Harris 2009). Quite often, such programmes invite the participants to share and work with their own stories of grief, trauma and loss. For example, Playback Theatre (Fox 2007) has been used to assist new arrivals to explore their personal stories and in so doing create therapeutic benefit. The approach, pioneered by Jonathan Fox and Jo Salas in the 1970s, emerged from a therapeutic and theatre base. It involves a group of performers and a facilitator (known as the conductor) who invites members of the audience to share stories that are then symbolically re-enacted for the teller:

> [t]rained actors and a musician act out life stories volunteered by audience members. It happens on a bare stage. There are no costumes, no scripts. Playback can happen in a traditional theatre, a classroom, a living room, or on the street. Telling the stories of everyday citizens

is central to Playback. (It) gives voice and visibility to especially those most often overlooked and ignored. (Fox 2007, p. 92)

Inspired by psychodrama and the oral traditions of indigenous cultures, Playback Theatre aims to preserve memory and offer a means for a group of people to bond. In Playback Theatre there is a direct connection between politics and healing in that healing or 'redressive' outcomes are emphasized within the process (Strawbridge 2000, p. 9).

The reliance on testimony demanded by Playback Theatre has been contested by a number of authors. For example, Thompson (2011) describes the use of testimonies in refugee theatre as problematic. One of the risks of this practice in a cross-cultural context is that the approach may be linked to trauma relief discourse in ways that have limiting and colonizing ramifications. Thompson (2011), drawing on an examination of theatre interventions in Sri Lanka after the 2004 Tsunami, argues that if theatre is only conceived of as a way to process traumatic memory, 'it is in danger of universalizing and presenting how people should respond to appalling incidents. Their options become restricted to a testifier and witness model that reduces the multitude of forms of encounter that may be generated' (p. 62).

Salverson (1999) also claims that an insistence on testimony in community-based theatre with refugee participants is problematic warning that this is a dynamic which can 'reinscribe a victim discourse that sustains the psychic residues of violent histories, codifying the very powerlessness they seek to address'. Theatre that aims to represent refugee experiences in a naturalistic way runs the risk of 'being caught in an aesthetic of injury that reproduces configurations of power' (Salverson 1999). If through the dramatic representations rendered by refugee storytelling the audience is invited 'to step into the shoes of the refugee, to empathize with her . . . then the refugee becomes an object of spectacle and the audience member- and, by extension, playwright, director and actors- offstage voyeurs' (Salverson 1999).

Dennis (2008) maps out some of these tensions in the context of a Playback Theatre project with refugee and asylum seekers in Brisbane,

Australia. This Playback Theatre performance took place in a particular historical context shaped by the then Australian government's immigration policies and the dismantling of multiculturalism in the early 2000s. In this setting, as Dennis (2008) observed:

> [t]he storytelling act reaches well beyond this performance. The experience refugees have of repeatedly telling their story, where they come to understand this act as a kind of currency, where each telling promises a move along the continuum from refugee to resident, means that there is an ambiguity in the value invested in the 'telling of a story' during the performance. (p. 361)

Dennis sees the potential for Playback Theatre to function as a bridge, where stories may be 'exchanged for entry into the new world; exchanged for access to a new future; exchanged for a chance to re-story a life that has been disassembled by war and terror' (pp. 366–7). This demands particular skill on the part of the Playback company who must be able to consciously balance the analytical/critical and artistic demands of the form. Dennis argues that it needs 'a kind of deliberate and thoughtful practice that repeatedly makes explicit who is there, who is missing, who has told, what voices are absent, what stories are absent, what assumptions we are making' (p. 367). This line of thought echoes that expressed by Salverson (1999) who suggests that 'performances which testify must explore form and content in ways which move beyond various binaries . . . and invite and retell the complex mix of fears and desires, abilities and injuries, that comprise subjecthood'.

Moving beyond an individual psychological focus

While this book is focused on participatory and process-based arts practice (e.g. no public performance or outcome), many of the issues related to intention, approach and representation of people from a refugee background are significant. How the arts practitioner's intention informs the approach surfaces in myriad ways through the practice.

Decisions about the design and selection of activities are underpinned by the values and beliefs of the practitioner. As we have discussed earlier, our approach was to concentrate on here-and-now stories and experiences relating to settlement and transition.

This strength-based approach grew out of the literature about early resettlement needs and the grounded experiences and perspectives of our partner organizations. Our aim was to draw on the resilience of participants through a strong pragmatic focus on enhancing language skills in order to better support the process of settlement. Where emotions or experiences surfaced we acknowledged and respected these, but didn't look to harness them into a testimonial story. There was a deliberate eschewing of, first, the assumption that all refugees are traumatized and, second, that re-telling and the re-performing of trauma or refugee stories would be of benefit with our participant groups. Burvill's invoking of Levinas philosophy is useful here again. In *Ethics and Infinity*, Levinas and Nemo proposed the idea that an ethical encounter is one that is active and responsive, a form of *saying* rather than *said*:

> [t]he saying is the fact that before the face I do not simply remain there contemplating it, I respond to it. The saying is a way of greeting the Other, but to greet the Other is already to answer for him. It is difficult to be silent in someone's presence; this difficulty has its ultimate foundation in this signification proper to the saying, whatever is the said. (Levinas and Nemo 1985, p. 88)

The decision to make our case studies participatory and process orientated was driven by a responsivity to the needs of each group. We did not explicitly take the decision to do participatory process-based work, but rather it was a response that emerged the more we listened and talked with community workers, participants and agencies. In fact it was a little like five researchers in search of a project. We spent many hours meeting with MultiLink workers and visiting a number of project groups. In many instances we felt the groups were high functioning and that there was no need for additional projects. In retrospect this perceived slowness and the time taken to listen to different voices within the community was an essential part of the process. For us this was a process of *saying* rather than an insistent *said*. A waiting. A silence. In the process what emerged was a more community rather than individually focused set of intentions for the practice.

The shift to a community-based focus connected with what Yohani (2008) argues is an ecological framework for practice that emphasizes hope and possibility. Drawing on the work of Lynch (1965) she describes hope as an active force. It is embedded in personal experiences and life contexts and involves action and the personal appraisal of action. It is nurtured in reciprocal relationships. Furthermore, Yohani (2008) sees a link between resilience and hope, and between creativity and hope, claiming that 'individuals who are able to hope, despite past challenges and unknown outcomes, are said to do well in life as they engage in a creative imaginative process that allows them to see beyond boundaries and live without absolutes' (p. 314).

While not focusing on the context of refugee resettlement, Winston (2013) also noted the place of hope in participatory drama practice stating that through participatory drama practice, those engaged had the opportunity to develop 'vocabularies of pleasure, hope, passion, emotion, experience and togetherness' (p. 135). Neelands and Nelson (2013, p. 17) extend this by referring, not only to hope, but to the claim that participation in applied theatre and drama can foster particular qualities of behaviour including co-operation, altruism, trust and empathy. Jeffers (2012, p. 137) extends this, claiming that further benefits include 'confidence building, encouraging social skills and challenging negative images'.

A further positive outcome of arts practice is the opportunities afforded to build positive communities. Neelands and Nelson (2013, p. 16) claim that there is evidence that participatory drama has the capability of facilitating 'the development of community among participants'. In the context of refugee resettlement, this has been the focus of a number of recent Australian projects. The purpose of many of these community arts projects is to empower those from refugee backgrounds to explore their role in a new setting and to build, understand and empathize among a diverse community of newcomers and members of the host society through creative collaborations. Such programmes aim to provide a forum for cross-cultural interaction between local communities and newcomers. The intention is that such a process will actively foster the development of community.

The combination of the literature on early settlement and consultation with community partners shaped the more community-focused approach of the practice we took. However, it wasn't until we started working in each of the contexts that the philosophical notions were converted into specific forms and approaches. In the next section, we would like to frame the practice that we will be exploring in this book through providing some background to the key arts approaches used across the three case studies. These were in broad terms: the application of process drama, arts-based conflict management through enhanced Forum Theatre and multi-arts approaches in community contexts. These will serve as introductions to the case studies and provide the reader with an overview of the approaches used.

Process drama

Although we use the term process drama within this book to describe the dramatic approach used within, other people, referring to the same practice, may use a different label, for example, educational drama, drama in education, interactive or improvisational drama. While it shares the key elements of other theatre events (role, focus, tension, symbol, metaphor, space, place, time, timing) process drama proceeds without a script and without a separate audience. It is an improvised and group art form and pedagogical approach involving a facilitator (often referred to as a teacher/artist) and a participatory group. It involves the participants and the facilitator working together to create and explore dramatic meaning.

The action of process drama is stimulated by a pretext. The pretext can take many different forms. For example, it might be an image, an object, a story or a fragment of a letter. For one of the dramas discussed in this book, the pretext took the form of a narrative about a robot from outer space that has landed on earth. The robot has lost their dog and is keen to locate him.

Supported by the facilitator, the participants explore the pretext and the meaning within and beyond it using a number of dramatic conventions. Those conventions require the participants to adopt a range of arts-worker positions at different times. While it is commonly accepted that process drama participants adopt role, (and could therefore be said to be operating as actors) they may also be variously engaged as writers, directors or perhaps designers. As well, they sometimes operate as spectators of each other's action. The conventions used within the process drama also include a variety of strategies that encourage interaction, communication and purposeful writing.

A strategy that is commonly used with process drama that is not necessarily adopted in other participatory drama practices is the use of teacher-in-role. The teacher adopts the stance of a fictional character from within the world of the drama and interacts with the participants from this position. O'Toole and Stinson (2013, p. 174) highlight how the use of teacher-in-role has significant impact because it diminishes the teacher's authority in relation to the children.

There are a number of different types of roles that can be adopted by the facilitator. The following two examples position the participants as more knowledgeable or more able than the teacher's role. For example, the teacher/facilitator might assume the role of someone who needs the help of the participants or perhaps they might take more of a middle position, such as the second in command who has some knowledge and authority but doesn't hold all the answers.

The text of a process drama is generated by the facilitator and participants. Together they manage the essential dramatic elements to explore and collaboratively create dramatic meaning. While an experienced facilitator will have some idea of how a particular group of participants might respond to the pretext, the outcome can be quite unpredictable. This is particularly so when a facilitator is working with a group less familiar to them. In our experience, the responses of participants within the fiction of the drama are also influenced by the actual life experiences of the participants.

Unlike theatre, there is no requirement to replicate the dramatic action for a season of performances. O'Neill (1995, p. xvi) notes:

> Like theatre, the primary purpose of process drama is to establish an imagined world, a dramatic 'elsewhere' created by the participants as they discover, articulate, and sustain fictional roles and situations. As it unfolds, the process will contain powerful elements of composition and contemplation, but improvised encounters will remain at the heart of the event as the source of its dramatic power.

As we mentioned in the introduction, a focus that developed for us as we negotiated how we might best support the needs of the new arrivals that we worked with was looking at ways participatory drama might support the development of their language skills. While we are unaware of a significant body of writing that looks at the use of process drama to assist the settlement of new arrivals, significant attention to its use with second and additional language learners (L2) has occurred.

Belliveau and Kim (2014) have recently examined the research literature from 1990 to 2012 that focused on the use of drama in L2 contexts. In a quest to understand what was known about the impact of using drama as a pedagogical approach in L2 contexts, they reviewed 'on-line teaching resources, position papers, scholarly articles and existing research findings'. They concluded thus:

> Educational drama invites learners into contexts where they are encouraged to spontaneously interact with their environment in meaningful ways (Cumico 2005; Eun and Lim 2009), experience different registers, styles, and discourses (Dodson 2000; Even 2011), and develop skills of discovery and interaction (Byram 1997), while collaboratively constructing imaginative worlds. (Bellieveau and Kim 2009, p. 11)

Like Bellieveau and Kim (2009), Stinson and Piazzoli (2013) acknowledge Kao (1998) as being the first person to study the use of process drama in L2 contexts. While Piazzoli noted that the desire to use the target language is higher, Kao also noted a significantly higher spontaneous use of the target language when using process drama. She attributed this to the presence of dramatic tension (the emotional energy) created through the participants' desire (in role) to achieve their characters' purposes.

While not working in an L2 context, O'Toole and Stinson (2013, p. 173) were focused on the use of process drama to develop oracy among a group of primary-aged children. They claimed that several contributing factors impacted on the development of oracy through the work. These included the nature of process drama as a dialogic pedagogy that encourages the children to talk and 'some specific characteristics of drama which support challenge and risk-taking in language'. They claim that the use of role and the particular dramatic context created are the activators of learning. The use of role allows changed use of language and changed status dynamics. The context creates opportunities for purpose.

Freire (1998, p. 72) called for an education that was not fixed. Rather, he wanted an education that was 'something constructed by people engaged together in life', an imagined possibility. The embodied and purposeful experiences of the process drama experience broaden the registers, styles and discourses that might otherwise be present in the L2 classroom. The participants develop skills of discovery and interaction. Process drama can offer the opportunities that Freire had hoped for.

As well as the claims about the value of using process drama in L2 and other language development contexts, we also saw potential in such an approach because it offers an opportunity to engage the children emotionally, physically and intellectually and it enables them to explore material that is relevant to them but that contains a degree of distance. The distance we refer to is an emotional distance that provides a degree of safety. As most drama practitioners would recognize, drama works at a level of remove.

However, to work at this level of remove, we must first intentionally find a point of connection. In one of the process dramas referred to in the next chapter, the sense of connection was offered by creating a character who is a new arrival in Australia. The required distance was created by making the character be a robot who has travelled from outer space and who is lost and in need of help. In this way, distance and empathy work together.

Forum theatre

As mentioned in the previous chapter, another participatory arts-based approach that has been used to consider a range of social issues (including resettlement) is Boal's Forum theatre. A number of Theatre in Education (TIE) companies have adopted this approach to explore refugee and homeless issues with young people. Day (2002) researched a London-based TIE project that involved young actors with personally relevant life experiences. This research adopted a case study methodology focusing on the Forum theatre workshops that took place in three, ethnically diverse, inner city London secondary state schools. It was 'quasi evaluative, focusing upon the experiences of the workshop by teachers and students and interactions between its participants' (p. 24). The study found that the use of Forum theatre gave students

> the opportunity to try out moral behaviour, which could potentially be applied to real-life situations. Students felt that the workshop enabled them to put themselves 'in other people's shoes', both the fictional characters in the workshop as well as actual people they knew at school. (p. 21)

The findings of this study however included the observation that the students were not given the opportunity or guidance to deepen the discussion with supported investigations and moral reflections in spite of the fact that the theatre company supplied a teacher's guide with many ideas for follow-up activities to the workshop. O'Toole et al. (2005) recognized that this can be a problem with the use of Forum theatre. They found that by extending the form to include the use of a range of process drama techniques, greater opportunities to deepen discussion and to consider the complex issues present in any situation were offered. They called their approach 'enhanced forum theatre'.

Enhanced Forum theatre is based on (but extends) Boal's earlier work. It has been revised and redeveloped over a number of years and combines approaches used in process drama with those contained in Boal's earlier approach. The inclusion of the process drama techniques allows deeper learning to occur in a way that counteracts some of the problems identified by Day (2002). In the following section a description of how enhanced Forum theatre is used by the *Cooling Conflict* team to explore issues of bullying and conflict is offered.

The process begins with the facilitator dividing the participant group (e.g. a class of students) into smaller groups of between five and eight people. Each of these smaller groups is then responsible for discussing and creating a play focused on an unresolved conflict or act of bullying that is serious and ongoing. The groups are instructed that one person will remain outside the action of the created plays to act as a facilitator (host or joker). The others assume the role of actors in the work. Their task is to create their plays in three scenes with each depicting one of the stages of conflict – *'latent, emerging and manifest'* (O'Toole et al. 2005, p. 93).

The participants are offered several different ideas about how they might choose a suitable story to depict. For instance, they may begin with a fictional story. Another suggestion is to use (but fictionalize) a story that has occurred to one of the potential spectators (e.g. children from another class). Another is to share their own stories and select one. However, when working with the personal stories of the group members they stress the necessity of creating distance and offer an approach that assists this process.

The participants form into pairs and each takes about 2–3 minutes to quietly and privately share with the other a conflict they have personally experienced that contains some unresolved tension. They are instructed that it must not be a story about someone else in the same class or that they will find traumatic to share. Following the initial telling, one person is designated as A and the other B. All the As are instructed to simultaneously tell their stories to B. The Bs then simultaneously tell the stories they have just heard back to A as though it is their own story. This is then reversed and B tells their story with A repeating it back to B, as though it is their own. Another step is sometimes added here with B, as the listener, assuming a different role, for example, they might become a good friend or counsellor who might offer advice from the perspective of the role adopted.

Each pair then chooses one of these stories before the pairs form into groups of about eight participants. These larger groups work simultaneously with each pair sharing the selected story with the others in their group. To maintain the anonymity, each person tells half the story as though it is their own. Once all the stories have been shared, each group selects one story that will become the basis of that group's enhanced Forum theatre. They are advised to choose a difficult conflict, one that is not easy to resolve.

Several steps are then used to fictionalize the event further. The names of the characters are changed. A role circle is used to offer each group member the opportunity to add a fictional element to the story that deepens the conflict. It also helps to make the story more complex and allows individuals to have a greater sense of ownership of the story. Once satisfied with the story the group make decisions about the motivation of each character and devise and rehearse a play that captures the conflict in three scenes that occur at least a week apart from each other. Various techniques drawn from process drama (e.g. hot seating) are used to add depth to the characters.

The host introduces the first scene, naming the work and explaining sufficient background information, for example, where the event is occurring to contextualize the scene for the audience. The first scene is then performed followed by further introductions by the host and the performance of the subsequent scenes.

Once all the scenes have been presented, the actors form a line at the back of the stage area and the host takes a hot-seat chair and places it close to the audience. The host invites the audience to select a character that they would like to find out more about. The selected character takes the hot seat and audience members ask them questions about the conflict. This may be repeated with several characters. Another technique sometimes used here is a truth-button. This is used when a character is being evasive and audience members want to know what they really think or feel.

With further depth created for the characters, the performance is shown again. This time the audience is instructed that they can stop the performance at any time and find out what a character is really thinking and feeling by calling for the actors to freeze. The audience member who has stopped the action will then be asked which character they want to know about. The nominated character then speaks 'exactly what is going through his/her mind at that moment' (O'Toole et al. 2005, p. 103). If the audiences request it, they can also hot seat any of the characters in the play at the end of each scene to interrogate the motives, attitudes or behaviours they revealed in a particular scene.

A further step that follows in the process also involves the audience stopping the action. This occurs in two ways and for two reasons. The first involves a spectator stopping the action because they can see an alternative way of behaving or responding that might help the situation. The person who has stopped the play is invited to enter the action and assume role of one of the characters who they believe could behave differently. The intention is that by doing this they might be able to de-escalate or resolve the problem from within. The second reason to stop the action is when a spectator (or the facilitator) witnesses behaviour that they think is unrealistic or implausible.

The next step in the process is that of mediation. With the scenes unlikely to have been resolved, the larger group forms into smaller groups of about five to six participants. Each group is asked to consider who from the scene might benefit from some form of mediation and who would be best placed to provide the mediation. Together they decide where and when this would take place and 'discuss and decide a strategy for addressing the conflict' (O'Toole et al. 2005, p. 107). Discussion of all the proposals occurs before the group selects the strategy that they think might be most useful and try it with the nominated character. This is followed by reflective discussion.

Obviously, the complex issues portrayed via Forum theatre are not easily solved. Rather, the form is a way to consider them. As Jackson (2005) noted about the 'Home and Away' project discussed by Day (2002),

> it was the differentiated voices (not only different viewpoints but different cultural and stylistic voices) that were foregrounded and that provided an experience that was unsettling and resisted simple interpretation. The dialogues within the play – aesthetically resonant and pedagogically challenging – stimulated and enabled the dialogic structure of the event as a whole; they fed the more wide-ranging dialogues that took place in every corner of the room during the group work and subsequently the forum. (p. 116)

In Jackson's view it is this quality of resisting neat conclusion that binds the pedagogic, the social and the aesthetic and generates an arts-based intervention that resonates with audiences. The value of this capacity for unsettlement needs to be appreciated. In the case study (Chapter 5) we were interested in adapting what we knew about the programme into a more complex multicultural group setting. The application of the Acting Against Bullying programme to a secondary school L2 group was not our first choice, but came about as a request from the teachers and the school. There were some very real issues about how the newly arrived young people were being perceived by the general (very multicultural-based) school students. There had been a number of incidents of bullying and violence against the language students. It was a key concern of the school and indeed the language unit was separated off from the main school by a newly erected fence and locked gate. The programme was therefore about building bridges between the language unit students and the main school. It was important that the participatory drama found ways to negotiate and promote different kinds of student–student relationships.

A multi-arts approach

The third case study (Chapter 6) explores the use of multi arts as an approach to support the cultural literacy of young people with a refugee background. The starting point for this approach was an interest in the potential of different styles and forms of arts-based participation, drama, poetry, visual arts, dance, music, digital arts in deepening an engagement with language and culture. Underlying this approach was an understanding that language learning is inseparable from a sociocultural context. We were interested in the interplay between multi-arts, language and learning. The case study is really a story about the ways in which the weave of integrating arts and learning sometimes worked and at other times didn't. The braid between different art forms, language curricula and the learning needs of the group were the tension points or thread of the practice. Sometimes the thread was too loose (eclectic and incoherent) at other times the looseness created an important learning space (moments of beautiful spontaneity and reflexivity). Of course sometimes the thread was too tight – the practice became like a classroom session – and lost its aesthetic drive.

There are a number of examples of different kinds of multi-arts approaches with individuals from a refugee background. Yohani (2008) describes a Canadian research programme that involved a small, culturally mixed group of children. They participated in a 10-week community-based early intervention programme, exploring the theme of hope in the context of their resettlement experiences. They engaged in creating collages, making quilts and taking photographs. The works created formed the data for the research project and were the focus of discussions about hope between the children and the researchers. This provided opportunities for rich exploration of the children's understandings of the concept of hope in a way that was child friendly.

It also offered the children the opportunity for reflection in a supportive environment.

After the quilts were finished, the children exhibited their work to the broader community. The element of exhibiting and sharing their art work with a local audience offered further opportunities for dialogue between adults and children and the wider community.

> The quilt became a medium for the children to share their learning and experiences beyond the programs centre. As such it became another example of the ecological value of this medium of research to transfer information to different groups. The process of sharing results with others can also be viewed as hope enhancing for the children, particularly since the research highlighted the important reciprocal nature of hope. Thus, sharing children's explorations of hope can have a two-fold outcome – enhancing hope by self-explorations as well as enhancing hope by sharing explorations with others. (Yohani 2008, pp. 317–18)

The Horn of Africa Arts Partnership Program was a recent Australian multi-arts partnership programme (Clark and Gilmour 2011) designed to improve intercultural understanding and build community. It involved the Centre for Cultural Partnerships (Faculty of the Victorian College of the Arts and Music, University of Melbourne) and the Horn of Africa Community Network Association. The latter is a community-based settlement organization supporting different Horn of Africa communities (specifically Ethiopia, Eritrea, Somalia and the Sudan) in Melbourne.

In this project, the collaboration between the two partner organizations was a critical starting point for the community cultural development model used. The initial negotiations between the project partners established that an empowerment model would be used to work with young people from Horn of Africa refugee communities. Practice would be based on a set of ethical principles and protocols, including 'respect, openness, and acknowledging the diversity of cultures, as well as a commitment to cultural exchange and to the discipline of arts practice and the principle of artistic determination' (Clark and Gilmour

2011, p. 61). In this way the principle that improved intercultural understanding is a 'key component of community sustainability' (Clark and Gilmour 2011, p. 60), was modelled in the way the project was designed and managed. This philosophy flowed through to the process of engaging with participants, and to the priority placed on building community leadership skills and experience within this group of young people from refugee backgrounds. As the authors explain:

> An intercultural approach goes beyond celebrating diversity to empowering mutual learning and growth. It seeks proactive engagement and interaction regardless of race and ethnicity. This process of proactive engagement was modelled in the project as it worked to build responsibility among the participants – for themselves, for the team, and for the process. In the framework of sustainable communities, they have become agents for integration and intercultural understanding. (Clark and Gilmour 2011, pp. 68–9)

The programme involved the creation of a theatre piece that combined a number of refugee stories, rather than focusing on one individual's narrative. This gave the participants the opportunity to place their own experiences in a wider context while remaining an engaging storytelling experience for the audiences. The authors assert that complicating and consciously reworking the process of testimony and empathy is a way to re-conceptualize refugee identity as something more than those represented in the stereotypes of victim or criminal. They explain:

> The challenge for this sort of theatre is to bear witness, but to do it in such a way that acknowledges the complexity of individual situations, that speaks to issues of power and, while not dismissing empathy, looks to find different role models for the encounter between audience and performer – role models that are more about acknowledging responsibility (or obligation) and individual freedom. (Clark and Gilmour 2011, p. 63)

The success of this project relied on the sustained involvement of the project team and their commitment to the principles of empowerment and intercultural understanding. The project moved through a series of phases over several years. Beginning in 2007 with weekly open-access workshops run by professional artists in dance, music and theatre, the activities expanded to include collaborative script development and a theatre performance, then led on to creative applications of digital media in 2009. Clark and Gilmour (2011) discuss Bhabha's idea of the productive capacities possible in a 'third' cultural space:

> [a] willingness to descend into that alien territory may reveal that the theoretical recognition of the split space of enunciation may open the way to conceptualizing an international culture based not on the exoticism of multiculturalism or the diversity of cultures, but on the inscription and articulation of culture's hybridity. To that end we should remember that it is the 'inter' – the cutting edge of translation and negotiation, the in between space – that carries the burden of the meaning of culture. It makes it possible to begin envisaging national, anti-nationalist histories of the 'people'. And by exploring this Third Space, we may elude the politic of polarity and emerge as the others of ourselves. (p. 56)

Wakholi and Wright (2011) also refer to the way participation in a multi-arts programme can create a space where new meanings that may support resettlement can emerge. They write about The African Cultural Memory Youth Arts Festival (ACMYAF). This Western Australian festival engaged participants in a range of arts activities including 'play, singing, dancing, drumming, storytelling, reflective journal writing, script writing, painting, cooking, role playing and acting, public speaking and memory exercises' (Wakholi and Wright 2011, p. 5). The festival was designed to offer participants opportunities to develop bicultural competence.

The project focused on using the arts to discover new knowledge about interventions that might support positive settlement outcomes. It had an orientation towards community action and participatory practice, shared ownership and connecting the learning to an awareness of 'social group issues like colonialism, globalization, migration, visibility, racism' (Wakholi and Wright 2012, p. 93).

UNIVERSITY OF WINCHESTER
LIBRARY

The focus on creating an opportunity for participants to re-negotiate meanings attached to linguistic signs and symbols is apparent in the way the authors articulate the motivation for coordinating this project. They explain:

> It was the researchers' intention to create a festival that would be both a research and an aesthetic space – a 'third space' (Bhabha 1994) away from the everyday western world – through which participants could explore issues relating to their cultural memory and identity. Bhabha (1994) used the term third space in his critique of modern notions of culture, his argument being that third space is produced in and through language as people come together and particularly as they resist cultural authority, bringing different experiences to bear on the same linguistic signs or cultural symbols. In the third space self-affirming knowledge is articulated in order to counter exclusive cultural narratives emanating from the dominant culture. (Wakholi and Wright 2012, p. 91)

Through a series of workshops, cycles of dialogue and performances, the festival offered the participants opportunities to explore cultural identities. Outcomes of the project included a group-devised play based on a fictional storyline exploring migration and identity, *The Real Deal*, and a comedy sketch called *Australian Oz Idol*, which drew playfully on the reality TV shows, *American Idol* and *Australian Idol*. The theatre festival had two major objectives. It aimed to offer young people an experience of cultural learning, and also to generate new knowledge about bicultural socialization. Wakholi and Wright (2012) argue that this form of socialization was facilitated through the appropriation of cultural symbols from ancestral culture, the maintenance of social networks across the globe and the incorporation of these into new cultural contexts.

We will explore how these ideas of multi-arts were explored in detail in Chapter 6, but the key rationale for this kind of braided, hybrid way of working is to explore multiple forms of expression and communication. The multi-arts approach explores how a participant responds to working with clay, what emerges from learning and devising a new dance routine, how drama and storytelling can be shaped by different styles and forms and how when these elements are brought together individuals can explore the complexities of form, content, communication and representation. The emphasis here is as much on the aesthetic quality and form of communication as the content. And this can be an important tactic in sidestepping the issue of a testimonial or monological approach to representing a refugee story.

Conclusion

In this chapter, we have outlined some participatory arts projects that are occurring in refugee resettlement contexts. Our focus has been the various claims of benefit present in the literature. We have discussed work that has as its intention healing, building hope, building strong communities, promoting social change, establishing mutual respect, overcoming racism and supporting active struggle for social justice. We have also briefly outlined the particular approaches that informed the work you will encounter in the coming chapters.

Looking to theatre to reflect and interpret lived experiences in the world offers unique opportunities. As Conquergood (2002) explains, 'in this way we are afforded the benefit of performance as a lens that illuminates the constructed, creative, contingent, collaborative dimensions of human communication; knowledge that comes from contemplation and comparison; concentrated attention and contextualization as a way of knowing' (p. 152). With these beliefs and the further hope that our particular approaches would positively support the resettlement processes of the new arrivals in our projects, we began our work.

Part Two

4

A Giant, A Robot and A Magic Man: Process Drama in the Primary Years

This chapter focuses on the project work that involved the youngest of our participants – children aged 8–12 years. Occurring within the context of their own primary school classrooms, the drama work described and analysed here spanned three distinct phases of action research including a pilot study, two further phases of action, each building on our learning in the previous phases. Penny Bundy, Julie Dunn and Nina Woodrow conducted the first phase, while the second was conducted by Penny and Julie with Nina moving on to work on the project being conducted in the TAFE context. Consistent with the overarching goals of the broader project, our purpose in working with these newly arrived children, their teachers and the broader school community was to explore how drama approaches, and more specifically those used within process drama, might be employed to support refugee settlement processes.

As the title of this chapter suggests, the drama work described here was not driven by the children's stories of home, of departure or even of arrival, but instead focused on tall tales and legends. Supported by the possibilities created by working in an artistic medium that privileges symbol and metaphor, we were able to explore fantasy worlds that were nevertheless deeply human ones, involving characters and situations that were at once distanced from the children's lived experience, yet close enough to offer a real sense of connection to human circumstances and the emotions that are generated by these. Across each drama then, the experiences of fictional characters like giants, robots and magic men were explored.

Initiated by pretexts that are often but not always narrative in nature, process drama work proceeds in a series of episodes where the participants, together with the facilitator, engage in a collaborative, lived experience. Involving a number of key strategies, including the adoption of role by both participants and facilitator, participants co-create a dramatic world through management of dramatic elements including time, space, place, symbol and tension. Importantly, a key aspect of the process drama approach is the balance offered between experience and reflection. However, unlike many other forms of dramatic activity, process drama operates without an external audience, while props and costumes are only used in a minimal way. In the absence of a script, participants are required to contribute to the ongoing work in a spontaneous and responsive manner, meaning that it is impossible to totally predetermine the direction the work will take. Its improvised nature requires immediate and unplanned responses from participants and facilitator alike. However, unlike some other forms of improvised drama, process drama experiences are usually guided by detailed planning, with the facilitator being responsible for structuring the work to create rich opportunities for the participants who simultaneously create and embody the narratives explored.

Later in this chapter, the process drama experiences developed within this project will be discussed in detail, but first, some background to the primary school project is offered, followed by an outline of six guiding principles that drove the work.

Background

Having determined from the outset of the broader study that we would create projects responsive to the needs of the community, expressed through our partner MultiLink, this particular sub-project took some time to identify. Initially we had considered working with even younger children within a community playgroup run by the MultiLink staff, but upon visiting the playgroup and spending time with the parents, grandparents, caregivers, children and staff there, we determined that our involvement might negatively impact on what was already a highly cohesive and engaging experience for all.

We therefore looked for other spaces and opportunities to 'value add' through drama. The local primary school, through discussions with its principal and the head of special education, soon emerged as one such space. With a student population of approximately 730, 18 per cent of whom are from a refugee background, this school is a key provider in the area of language support for newly arrived children (aged 5–12 years). Some 75 per cent of students don't speak Standard English at home (school website), while the Index of Community Socio-Educational Advantage (ICSEA) (Barnes 2011) reveals that 53 per cent of families fall into the bottom quarter of this index, against a nationwide figure of 25 per cent (Australian Curriculum and Reporting Authority 2013).

In asking us to partner with them in this project, the school administrators established that one of their key goals was to identify approaches to the teaching of English that might enhance existing practices and additionally hoped that the research might serve to support staff in the application of these. However, and more importantly, the school team were keen to give the children directly involved in the project the opportunity to engage in learning experiences that might be fun, and that through this enjoyment the children might have the chance to discover new ways to see themselves as learners.

For our part, we were also committed to these goals, but in keeping with the overarching project, were also interested in broader aspects of settlement. Of course, like the school staff, we saw control over language as being a critical tool for individuals needing to establish themselves in a new cultural space, but we hoped that our specific dramatic approach might also support other aspects of resilience which Sarig (2001, cited in Doran 2005) has identified as including a sense of belonging, control over situations, the development of relevant skills, maintaining optimism and confidence to undertake positive challenges, and self-confidence.

We also had the additional goal of hoping to learn more about the challenges of using process drama with beginner language learners, especially within a context where there was no shared language to fall back on. As such, we were anxious about how we might work and wondered: would we have the skills to manage this challenging context? Would the children and their parents, with their diverse experiences, cultural backgrounds, educational experiences and refugee journeys, respond to drama as a learning medium? Would the constraints of the curriculum impact on our approach? Would we be able to locate materials as starting points for our drama that would connect to the children's lives sufficiently to enable them to engage? And perhaps most importantly, would we be able to ensure that the drama work 'protected' the children, that it did no harm in terms of their emotional needs?

Within this chapter then, we will tell the story of our time working with the children of this community. All aged between 9 and approximately 12 years of age, each child had his or her own unique arrival story, with countries of origin including the Sudan, Congo, Rwanda, Burundi, Myanmar (Burma), Laos, El Salvador, Macedonia and Thailand. The diversity of first languages was even greater, with children from individual countries such as Myanmar (Burma) speaking multiple languages. It should also be noted that a small number of the children in the various groups we worked with were immigrants rather than refugees, however in our research approach we made no attempt to differentiate between the children based on their arrival stories. Across all phases of the study, the children we worked with had all been resettled for less than 12 months, with some having come directly from the limbo spaces of refugee camps. Although not zones of direct conflict, these camps were nonetheless close enough for the children to have experienced some of the trauma of displacement that comes with war. With starkly contrasting levels of schooling experience and therefore literacy in their first language, the differences between the language and academic skills of the children were quite marked, although all would be considered beginner English language users. Indeed, in a couple of cases, the children appeared to have no English at all when they first joined us.

The chapter will also examine the experience of the children's teachers, for within this highly supportive school environment, it was the commitment of these adults that made our research possible, value adding to our approaches through the application and modification of their own.

In offering this material, our hope is to open up new dialogues about the learning needs of newly arrived refugee children and the pedagogies that might be used to engage, excite and support their settlement journeys. In particular, we aim to introduce to these dialogues a discussion of the possibilities offered by the application of process drama structures and strategies. In the following sections then, we will attempt to provide a snapshot view of what the work looked like, while also giving voice to the children and their teacher by drawing on their responses to it.

Guiding principles

The six principles offered here informed almost every aspect of our work in this project, for inherent within each of them are implications for practice. They emerged from our engagement with the refugee studies literature, our meetings with the MultiLink and school teams and our experiences as drama practitioners. Later in this chapter we will return to these principles as we examine the project outcomes.

1. Each child is an individual, with his or her own unique story, skills and ways of experiencing and understanding the world.

This philosophical position might seem to be fundamental within all educational contexts, but in the case of this project it gains more weight, for it is aimed at resisting the contrasting position that might seek to allow the term 'refugee' to define these children. Like Rotus (2004, p. 52), we believe that the term refugee is often used to 'smooth over differences within the group it designates', creating a situation that denies the highly individual nature of each child's experience. This 'smoothing over' ignores the fact that each child arrives under different circumstances, bringing with them their own unique personal and family histories. It also smoothes over differences in their learning needs, keenly influenced by their particular and highly varied educational experiences. These varied educational opportunities were particularly significant within this project where experiences had been uneven. For example, while some children had enjoyed solid educational experience and as such had made progress towards literacy in their first language, others had been offered no formal learning opportunities prior to arrival. For these children in particular, the challenges were greater, for as Cranitch notes (2011 p. 265), 'English language acquisition for learners with a history of disrupted education and who arrive at school essentially preliterate, is a slow process where progress needs to be measured in small increments'.

In addition, there were of course gender and cultural differences between these children, with their countries of origin having an impact on both of these. Finally, and importantly within the context of this study, this individuality was also apparent in terms of their experiences of play, drama and storytelling, including their confidence working in this medium and their willingness to take a risk within it.

2. Trauma stories or approaches that adopt deficit models need to be resisted.

Relating to the overarching notion of acknowledging and celebrating the unique nature of each individual, was our determination, as noted in Chapter 1, to resist any work focused on trauma stories or indeed any positioning of our work as some type of therapeutic 'intervention'. This perspective appears to be in stark contrast with much of the literature reviewed earlier in this book, where arrival stories have often dominated, or where refugee children and young people have been positioned as victims, bereft of hope and in need of 'healing'. Such approaches are based on the presumption of trauma – a presumption that can lead to an 'otherizing' of these children and a sense that they are 'strangers that we have to deal with, living in a liminal zone amongst – and yet not-quite-amongst – us' (Rotus 2004, p. 52).

From our perspective, these perceptions have too often resulted in practitioners opting to work in ways and with materials that are considerably different from those included when working with children in more mainstream, non-refugee projects. However, Hallahan and Irizarry (2008, p. 125) have warned that these approaches have a tendency to 'romanticise resilience', and argue that to overcome this possibility, children from refugee backgrounds should be provided with 'normalizing' social experiences, especially those that 'stress the importance of everyday life and of life-affirming ideologies'.

Within this project then, our goal was to reject deficit perspectives, and instead, to create work that positioned our participants as capable and competent learners. We therefore took the optimistic view offered by Papadopoulos (2007) that difficult experiences can sometimes help people 'reshuffle their lives and imbue them with new meaning' (p. 304), providing impetus and motivation that may not be present in individuals who have progressed through their lives with less disruption and fewer challenges. Such an assumption fortunately appeared to be supported by the children's responses, for across all phases of our project they appeared to be forward focused, keen to learn and holding exciting aspirational goals for their futures.

Of course, we are not suggesting here that there was no one in the various groups we worked with who needed therapeutic support and are clearly not rejecting the importance of such processes. However, given our involvement in these children's lives as visiting drama educators, we adopted the view that the most appropriate course of action for us was to approach the work and indeed the children themselves in the same manner as we would with any other class of beginner drama students. In doing this, we tried to remain true to our beliefs about how best to manage the elements of drama in action, and about structuring to achieve engagement and connection, with a key component of this being the importance of working aesthetically.

As such, we aimed at all times to adopt approaches and select materials based on our perceptions of their artistic and educational value. Of course, we understood that adjustments in both of these aspects would be required due to the children's varied educational experiences, their personal life experiences, the absence of a shared language in the classroom and most significantly the children's beginner English language learner status. However, we were supported in developing these adjustments by the latest literature from the rapidly increasing body of work exploring process drama as a vehicle for additional language learning (Kao and O'Neill 1998; Liu 2002; Stinson and Freebody 2008; Piazzoli 2012; Rothwell 2012; Dunn and Stinson 2012; Piazzoli and Stinson 2013).

3. Language is power and as such is a key aspect of resilience.

Reinforcing the philosophical position outlined above is the view offered by Marlowe (2010, pp. 195–6) that the source of resilience resides outside the trauma story, being located instead within each individual's 'culture, history, values, stories and traditions, along with dreams and aspirations for the future'. With this perspective in mind, we adopted the position that resilience is something that is revealed rather than developed (Goodman 2004) and that opportunities for children and young people to exercise agency (Pufall and Unsworth 2004) are a key means of achieving these revelations. However, agency is, at least in part, exercised when your ideas are given a voice, and to do this effectively, control over language is necessary.

Haseman and O'Toole (1990, p. vi) have previously argued that language is power, and that control over spoken language is a key means of overcoming social and economic disadvantage. They note: 'The ability to manage and not be managed by language is one way to overcome the inequities of society'. As such, they are expressing the view that language and its acquisition offers possibilities denied without it. O'Toole also usefully reminds us (1991) that the vast majority of human communication occurs in face-to-face contexts, where the spoken word is accompanied by gestures, facial expression and body language.

For this reason, we wanted to apply a pedagogy that would give our participants confidence as language learners.

4. Children's language learning is supported when learners are empowered and where the pedagogical approach offers new ways for participants to see themselves as learners.

Belief in this principle underpinned everything we attempted to do within this project. Our goal was to create a learning context with the potential to empower and engage the learners, supporting them to explore ideas and language in embodied ways. We also wanted to apply a pedagogy that would offer participants new ways to see themselves as learners (O'Connor 2013). Drama was therefore a good fit, for it is a pedagogy that creates a landscape for learning characterized by emotion and empathy, the imagination, embodiment, the importance of the fictional context, identification with roles, the application of narrative, collaboration, open-endedness, juxtaposition and reflection (Dunn and Anderson 2013, p. 299).

Through the creation of shared experiences that sit betwixt and between the actual world and the dramatic one, drama opens up opportunities for ideas to be explored in a low-risk environment. This low-risk environment, according to Cahill (2013, p. 180), is enabled because drama makes use of fictional stories and scenarios that, for its participants, are 'theirs and not theirs', providing opportunities for those involved to contest and resist dominant discourses and to bridge the gap between knowledge and its application within social and relational contexts.

By operating in this way, drama has the potential to simultaneously address transcultural and intercultural awareness/literacies, suggesting goals well beyond the development of language alone. In addition, as a form that engages participants at both a cognitive and an affective level, emotions play a key role. The activation of these emotions tends to ensure that the drama experiences, and indeed the language used to structure them, are vividly recalled making it an important pedagogy within any learning context, but especially one that targets language learners.

A further characteristic of process drama is that it allows for shifts in status between teacher and learner. Through its strongly oral approach, process drama specifically provides rich and contextualized opportunities for language learners to use vocabulary and language structures within authentic contexts. For this reason, Yaman Ntelioglou (2011, p. 598), who works with newly arrived adult immigrants in Canada, points out that 'drama pedagogy has the potential to provide a rich context in which to use the networks of signs that exist in real life'. Here both the verbal and non-verbal modes of communication are reflected. As such, Beatty (2009) argues for drama pedagogies to be applied more widely within work involving all English language learners, but especially for recently arrived refugee children.

In recent work in Hong Kong, To, Chan et al. (2011) have provided a summary of the benefits they believe arise from using a process drama approach for the teaching of additional languages. They summarize these benefits as: motivation to learn, confidence in speaking, improvement in writing, using language in context with purpose, richer means of expression, engagement of students of different abilities, more active participation, better teacher–student relationships and more supportive and appreciative attitudes among students (p. 524).

Stinson and Piazzoli (2013, p. 218) have also explored the value of drama for additional language learning, focusing on the features of drama that make it effective. In particular they have identified how specific elements of drama may be manipulated to activate agency in the learners, including how role, focus and tension operate. In relation to role, they note that drama reverses the traditional hierarchy of status, contributing to a more authentic context for learning, while focus and tension work together to create a sense of urgency in the communication. They suggest therefore (p. 218) that the 'manipulation of these elements contribute to create a favourable condition for self-expression, and a willingness to take initiative in the target language'.

Finally, beyond the more basic goal of developing language skills, drama offers opportunities to reveal the development of resilience through independent thinking, critical thought and self-knowledge (McPherson 2010).

5. Acknowledgement of and respect for the existing practices of the school community context and its inherent constraints.

As visitors within this school community, it was important that in all aspects of our work we showed respect for its existing practices and acknowledged its inherent constraints including the organization of classes, the structure of the school day, the requirements of the mandated curriculum, staffing arrangements, approaches to research and even the available physical spaces. At times, these practices extended the challenges for us as researchers, but with this principle in mind, our goal was to be as flexible and respectful as possible, absorbing these challenges as simply part of the context.

The first of these challenges related to the organization of class groups. Student groupings involving children in need of English language support are somewhat unique in their arrangement in the local school system. Here the special education unit employs specially trained language teachers to work with groups of multi-aged children, with two distinct groupings being used. The first involves students in Years 1–3 (5–8 years of age) while a second includes students in Years 4–7 (8–12-year-olds). Within these broader bands, individual students progress through various groupings according to their language development and as required to accommodate the constant stream of new arrivals. This structure, while effective in terms of the school and its needs, also meant that additional challenges were thrown up for the research as new children continuously joined the group, while others who were committed to the work and making good progress left us for other classes. The specific nature of this challenge in relation to the newcomers was twofold. These children not only had little or no English language skills, but also had not established a connection to the work, its narrative or characters. In addition, as all children attend some mainstream sessions with others of their own age, including swimming, physical education, music lessons and school assemblies, finding blocks of time to work with all students in the group was an additional challenge.

The decision to work with the older, most recently arrived children was also a factor of the existing practices of the school, for quite appropriately, the principal had expressed a strong preference for us to work with the teacher who showed the keenest interest and commitment to partnering with us in this research work. For the pilot phase, the teacher who expressed this interest worked with newly arrived children in the year 4–7 grouping. Fortunately, when she was promoted to higher duties and was no longer working directly with a class, we were able to partner across the two remaining phases of the project with another teacher working with this same group. A highly skilled and enthusiastic partner in our research, we will refer to her by the pseudonym Katie within this chapter.

Other constraints also need to be acknowledged, including the pressures the staff work under in terms of national benchmark testing. Not surprisingly, given the diversity of languages, arrival stories and educational and socio-economic backgrounds of the students who make up the overall population of our partner school, its results on the NAPLAN sit well below the national average across almost all fields tested and in all age groups. Heavily influenced by the requirement that children sit these tests after just one year of settlement and language instruction classes, these results nevertheless lead to pressures being placed on all teachers in this context, including those working in the English as a Second Language Unit (ESL unit). Fortunately, other published indicators paint quite a different picture of the school's effectiveness, with the most recent independent teaching and learning audits (Department of Education and Training 2012) of the school revealing a 'high' result in seven of the eight areas reviewed (improvement agenda, data analysis, learning culture, targeted resources, teaching team, curriculum delivery and effective teaching), while an 'outstanding' result was recorded in relation to the final area, differentiated learning.

This audit result clearly indicates that the school is offering a learning and teaching environment that is well matched to student needs, but nevertheless, the pressure to improve results in the NAPLAN tests remains as a pressure point for teachers and was therefore a factor we needed to consider when seeking time with the children.

Other contextual features were also important and are related to broader curriculum demands. For example, while teachers within the ESL unit are given some leeway in terms of how they address the mandated curriculum, there is nevertheless the expectation that the children will engage with all areas of learning, including among others, English, Mathematics, Science, History, The Arts and Information Communication Technologies (ICTs). Consideration of the last of these ICTs would eventually prove to be quite critical to our work, with a real effort being made to incorporate the use of computers and iPads into the drama. As will be noted below, in the first phase work the application of these technologies would prove to be highly useful, serving to enhance engagement, motivation, language and even learner agency. However, in the second phase, their value was limited if not potentially a negative to our work. Nevertheless, as a critical component of the school's learning policy, their incorporation is a useful example of our attempts to show respect for existing practices.

6. The importance of partnerships and reciprocity in research.

This final principle relates to our desire for this school-based research to be a reciprocal process, creating opportunities for mutual engagement and learning. An important component of this is an awareness of the cultural and social capital all participants, including the children, bring to the work. For example, in relation to the children, it was important for us to recognize that while they were in need of support to develop their English language skills, many of them were already multilingual language users, with a mother tongue as well as some additional language learnt during their refugee camp/transition experiences. Additionally, it was essential that we recognized the expertise of all members of the school staff, including the community liaison officers, assistant teachers and parents.

A key aspect of this is the acknowledgement that our work in this school community was only a very small part of these children's educational experience, with the broader community being responsible for creating the nurturing and supportive context we were fortunate enough to enter. This educational context, to a significant extent, frames these young people's lives, creating a unique cultural space for their learning. Positioned somewhere between the children's home culture and their experiences within the cultures of the broader community, this school appeared to offer its students a relatively risk-free environment in which to engage. We therefore wanted to learn about how such environments are constructed and how learning is structured and managed within them.

As such, a partnership approach to the research was critical, with a close working relationship with the children's teachers being required. As part of this partnership, across all phases of this work, the drama lessons were deliberately and comprehensively supported through the application of a range of established language and literacy strategies. These strategies, designed by the classroom teachers, were offered between the drama sessions and keenly influenced the outcomes achieved, serving as well to keep the learners connected to the dramatic world between sessions.

With its rich diversity of clientele, the school attracts a significant number of researchers, with several projects operating within the school at any one time. However not all of these projects are perceived by the teaching staff as being a positive, with Katie, our partner researcher noting within her interview that a lot of this research is of the 'take' variety that does little to value add to the school community. We were therefore keen for our work to be seen as the 'giving' kind, offering something of value to our participants and the school community more broadly.

Research approach

These principles underpinned the research design in a significant way, while the key learnings developed through the pilot study were also important. This pilot study was originally designed to identify the possibilities and challenges of using process drama as the pedagogical approach with beginner language learners from a range of cultural groups, and with no shared language other than the slowly emerging English. However, it also served to reveal important insights about what might and might not be realistic in terms of the data-collection process.

The eventual shape of the project emerged then as involving two phases of data collection, each involving weekly visits of 2-hour duration across almost a full school term (8 weeks). Separated by the long summer break, these two phases involved two groups of children, with the second group having a marginally better grasp of English. A small group of about four children participated across both phases, while two children participated across three (including the pilot study).

Within these phases, a range of data was collected: video and still photographic recordings of all sessions, artefacts of children's work and our planning, teaching resources, audio files of children's verbal responses to set tasks, web-based resources (both ours and the children's), audio recordings of interviews with the phase 1 and 2 teacher and student interviews – with one set being conducted immediately following the phase 2 work, while another set was conducted with the available phase 1 students 1 year after the completion of our work with them. These latter interviews were designed to capture the children's memories of working with us and offered useful insights not possible at the time of the work due to the children's extremely low English vocabulary and confidence at the time.

A significant additional source of data was the audio recordings of the reflective conversations completed at the conclusion of each session. Involving members of the research team present at a given session, they captured reflections on the work completed, children's responses and ideas for future directions in the work. From these, vignettes of action were created, with some of these being offered below as a means of capturing the essence of key moments as they occurred.

Each session involved two and sometimes three researchers, with one generally adopting the role of drama facilitator, while the other/s took major responsibility for overseeing the data-collection process. At times however, two researchers were directly involved in the teaching process, especially when the children were working in small groups, and on these occasions the quality of the video data was variable. This variability was partly due as well to the size of the spaces we worked in, with all of the classrooms being very small. In addition, as the classrooms were set up with desks and chairs, these also had to be accommodated, leaving an even smaller space in which we could conduct the drama work. Given the presence of the children (usually around 15 to a class), the children's teacher, the teaching assistant and the two or three research team members, the room was quite crowded and often chaotic.

The pilot study – A giant

From the outset of this primary school study, we were aware that there was nothing in the research literature about using drama as a pedagogical vehicle in such a challenging context, and were therefore hoping to 'try it out', being ready to abandon it completely should the reality of working in this way prove to be too complex. However, in spite of our concerns, it became clear immediately that the children were responding very positively to the approach and were highly engaged by this way of working.

Discussions with the children's teacher prior to commencing the work had revealed that in spite of their age (8–12 years) these newly arrived children were interested in fairy tales. As such, she suggested that they would respond positively to a drama involving a giant. Having previously developed and facilitated on many occasions a drama about a *Giant who threw Tantrums* (O'Toole and Dunn 2002), a modified version of this plan was selected for the pilot study.

Our initial fears were that the language demands of the short story that initiates this drama would be too challenging for the children, and for this reason, it was adapted to include greater repetition and a keener focus on the use of images. These two ideas proved to be successful, with the children engaging immediately in exploration of the story of a young boy who comes across a giant throwing tantrums at the top of a mountain. His endeavours to get the townspeople to believe this tale are at first unsuccessful, but eventually a giantologist is brought into the town to help the people resolve the situation.

Somewhat surprisingly, and unlike the responses generally generated by this pretext, the children involved in the pilot study immediately felt empathy for the giant's situation, suggesting that the cause of his tantrum throwing was most likely to be that he was cold, had nowhere to live and was undoubtedly hungry. They were therefore very careful in terms of creating a plan to capture him, determining that one effective way might be to lure him by cooking sausages and then to use a net and hypodermic injection to calm him down.

The plan outlined below was created by the children (in role as the people living in the town) to support the hopelessly inept giantologist (Julie using the teacher-in-role strategy). However, as the drama

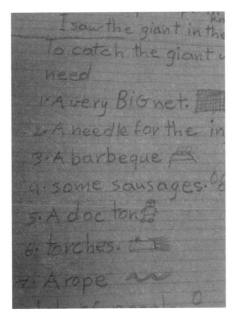

Figure 1 The children's plan to catch the giant.

continued, the children were challenged to review their collaboration with this giantologist based upon a letter written by the Giant asking them to reconsider their plans (especially the use of the injection!) and instead to see the situation from his perspective.

Some children were persuaded by this appeal, others not so. The following transcript excerpt reveals some of what happened when the giantologist met with the townspeople following the arrival of the letter:

Giantologist: So do you still want me to catch the giant?

Children: (*variously*) Yes, No!

Giantologist: Well which is it?

Child 1: The giant said, 'Why are you so mean?'

Giantologist: Ok, but do you still want me to catch the giant or not?

Child 2: Yes . . . because he's no good . . . he breaks everything . . . he use a tree to hit my garden . . . and he threw my house . . . and into my garden . . . and throw my computer!

Giantologist: He did all of that? Oh dear. And what about you, do you still want me to catch the giant?

Child 3: No, he is my friend . . .

Giantologist: So how many of you want me to keep doing this job? (*Counts*) Three! What about the rest of you?

Child 4: We can do it. We do a good job.

Giantologist: Oh so you think you can do this without me?

Child 5: Yes, because the giant like us and the giant said why are you so mean. We don't want to do anything to him . . .

Giantologist: So you've changed your mind?

Children: Yes!

Giantologist: I thought we had a deal! Now only three people in the town want to do this thing? Don't you want to make a trap with a big net, and sausages, and a torch?

Child 3: The giant has feelings . . . he sent us a letter.

Giantologist: Giants can't write letters!

Child 4: Yes giants can!

Child 5: The giant's scared of needles.

Giantologist: Are you serious, do you believe that?

Children: Yes.

Giantologist: Come on, he's as tall as the forest, why would he be scared of needles? You don't believe that do you?

Children: Yes!

Child 6: We want to help the giant.

Clearly, some of the children were struggling with where their loyalties lay, with possibly their own experiences of injections, administered upon arrival, driving their change of heart in relation to this troubled character.

To provide a satisfactory conclusion to the drama work, the children were invited to create a digital photo story that retold the events of the drama, using images and recordings of their voices. In creating these photo stories, the children were also encouraged to create a suitable ending. The bonus of this strategy was that it also served as a powerful language review, helping the teacher to identify the learning that had occurred through the drama.

This pilot study was therefore an extremely successful experience for everyone involved, with the learnings generated having a significant impact on our work. For example, it was clear from the children's responses, the talk and writing produced and the school's enthusiasm for participation to continue, that the approach had been a success. In addition, useful insights were gained into how existing drama experiences and approaches could be adapted for work with beginner language learners, while the value of technology as a supporting framework was also revealed. Interestingly, one of the two children who remained with us across all three phases of this project indicated that this had been her favourite drama, with her level of recall, almost 18 months after its conclusion, being remarkable.

Phase 1 – A robot

With a new partner teacher to work with and a mostly new group, we began this first official phase of the project. Our first official visit to the

ESL2 classroom offered us the opportunity to meet the children and familiarize ourselves with the space we would be working in. Katie, our partner teacher, had worked with the children prior to our arrival to create 'visual' family trees that the children happily, but shyly, shared with us.

She informed us that the class were working on a 'space' theme and asked us to contribute to this work in some way. As well, she indicated that she would like us to once again include the use of technologies in the work.

Following this visit we (Penny, Julie and Nina) met to consider how we might create a process drama experience that would match this brief while also offering rich opportunities for language learning. We needed to create a fictional context that would allow the children to apply the English language skills they already had, while building on these through authentic interactions. We also needed to create a starting point or pretext that would be of interest to the children, one that would drive the action of the drama and would also place them in empowered positions as language learners.

We had little knowledge of the specific background experiences of these children beyond knowing their countries of origin and the information provided in the family trees they had created for us. For this reason, we wanted to be careful that we didn't select a dramatic context that might trigger traumatic memories and determined that the best way of avoiding this outcome was to create a character and a story with plenty of emotional distance. However, in order for process drama work in any context to be effective, a sense of connection is needed, and we therefore understood that the characters and situations we explored would need to offer some resonances to the children's own experiences.

With all of these ideas in mind, we determined that it would be necessary to create a pretext from scratch, eventually agreeing that we would begin by introducing the children to the story of a robot called Rollo who travels to Earth from the distant planet of Buttonridge, accompanied by her robot dog, Sparky. With her spaceship safely landed in the local area, Sparky promptly runs away, leaving Rollo alone and understandably very upset. The search for her missing dog sees her arrive at the door of ESL2 – alone, in a strange new world and feeling very confused.

To introduce the children to these ideas, we decided that the immediate use of teacher-in-role would be the best approach, with one of us assuming the character of Rollo by donning a rudimentary costume created out of a silver, painted cardboard box. We then developed the pretext further, adding another layer that would help us to raise the status of the children in relation to the teacher's role: the fact that Rollo spoke no English. In fact, as a robot, she spoke no known human language.

By positioning Rollo in this way we were hoping that the children would identify with her situation, while also providing opportunities for them to be empowered as language experts, given that each of them, irrespective of their experiences and duration of settlement, had more English than she did!

For the first session we decided that Julie would lead the lesson and that Penny would assume the role of Rollo. Nina worked as the researcher. We moved the desks aside as much as we could to clear a space in which to work. After some brief name games which helped us get to know the children and also had them working bodily in the space, we talked to them about drama and about pretending. We tried some very simple role activities that required us all to pretend. After that, we introduced the costume that we had created for Rollo and explained that when Penny stepped inside the box, she would assume the role of Rollo, also explaining that the robot had an 'on' and an 'off' switch.

As soon as Penny stepped into the box, the children began to playfully experiment with turning Rollo on and off! However, once persuaded to leave her turned on, the children learnt three key things about Rollo: she did not speak or understand English, she was very, very sad and she wanted their help. Their initial task then was to attempt to communicate with her in order to find out what was upsetting her and driving her strong desire to engage with them. Having tried (and failed) to communicate with her in English, with the support of Julie and their classroom teacher, they tried a range of other languages familiar to the children. They spoke to her in each of their mother tongues, even trying a little French and German, but she understood nothing.

Prior to commencing the drama, we determined a device that we would use to let the children teach Rollo the vocabulary she would need to communicate with them – that Rollo could learn English words (and their meaning) when the children wrote them on yellow post-it notes, attached them to the robot costume and taught her to pronounce them. The children readily accepted the pretence of this device and took great delight in introducing her to new words and correcting her intentional errors in pronunciation.

Having accepted this device, Rollo was switched off as the children worked together to determine what questions they wanted to ask her. The answers mattered to them. They really wanted to know who she was, where she was from, why she was upset and why she was in their classroom. They worked singly, in pairs and in small groups to create the 'sticky' labels they would need to teach her the words needed to ask their questions. One boy independently approached Rollo with his bundle of words, teaching Rollo one word at a time: how, did, you, get, here.

Figure 2 How Rollo came to Earth.

In response Rollo drew a picture on the board of how she had travelled by spaceship from another planet. There was a small dog in the image too.

By the end of the first lesson, the children had taught Rollo (and for many, learnt themselves) the following words: am, America, Australia, are, Black, came, car, cat, colour, come, did, do, doing, dog, family, from, get, here, how, I, in, is, Laos, like, long, lost, moon, no, old, red, rocket, Rollo, Sparky, take, the, to, 12, week, what, where, which, white, who, with, write, yes, you, your. For Penny, in role as Rollo, trying to remember which words she was meant to know and which she didn't was quite challenging.

Eventually the class learnt that Rollo had come to Earth from her distant planet with her very naughty robot dog Sparky, who had run away. Initially the children focused on ways they might find, trap and capture the missing robot dog. They drew their ideas. They wrote their ideas. They enacted their ideas. They became television journalists interviewing the local people about the spaceship sighting and the missing dog. In the process, they developed real empathy for him and his plight, with one child writing:

I think Sparky is at Kmart. He is looking for Rollo and Keyboard. Sparky is so hungry. Sparky look for any food. Sparky is NO have many.

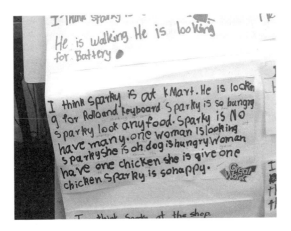

Figure 3 An example of the children's writing.

> One woman is looking at Sparky. She is no dog is hungry. Woman have one chicken. She is give one chicken. Sparky is so happy.

This empathy was heightened through the use of technology which allowed us to interact with the children between our visits to the classroom. As the children suggested locations where they thought Rollo might find her missing dog, we would create photos of the dog in those locations and email them to the children as mischievous postcards sent by him. As such, they received a variety of postcards from Sparky, including Sparky at Kmart, Sparky in the fridge, Sparky walking down the road, Sparky meeting 'Earth dogs' and Sparky undertaking research into planetary travel.

To heighten the children's engagement, and to extend opportunities for further language development, we also introduced a computer program called 'Xtranormal'. We used this program to introduce new characters into the drama, with the first of these being Rollo's quite cross robot mother called Keyboard. In her first contact with the children she sent them an animated message that introduced the idea that Rollo had in fact taken the family spaceship without permission. Her message to the children was that she was seeking their help to retrieve

Figure 4 Sparky undertaking research and meeting an Earth dog.

this spaceship and indeed her daughter. In response, the children were offered the opportunity to create their own digital characters to reply to Keyboard, choosing a voice for their characters and creating short animations.

While some, not surprisingly, chose characters from the library available within this program that reflected their sense of self (soccer players or modern newsreader women), others were more playful in their selections, with some opting for a character that sounded like and resembled the Queen of England. In creating these messages, the children drew on the language that had been explored across the various sessions, while the motivation to engage in these written tasks was fuelled by the joy they appeared to feel as participants in these novel learning experiences. In addition, the empathy they felt for both Sparky and Rollo was continuing to grow, with the children being very defensive of Rollo in their messages to her mother.

Following each of the sessions we met as a team to reflect on the work just concluded and to plan for the following session. Within these reflections we necessarily acknowledged those times when our approaches failed – where the children did not engage with the work

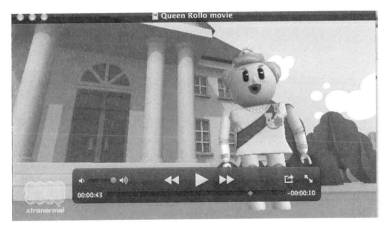

Figure 5 One of the children's animated images.

or where their language responses were limited. The transcript below highlights one of these occasions and relates to a segment of one lesson where the children were asked to imagine how their animated messages might have been received back in Buttonridge and then to create freeze-frames showing these responses. This quite abstract and overly complex task was not at all successful, and the following reflective conversation between Penny and Julie capture discussions relating to this failure.

> **Penny**: This was a failure because we weren't modelling enough here.
> **Julie**: And because the language demands were too high.
> **Penny**: Yes, the language demands were incredibly difficult . . . and this task was not where their heads were at.
> **Julie**: Yes, you're right they didn't care what Keyboard was thinking when she got the message. . . .
> **Penny**: Yes, and neither were they engaged by the character of Keyboard in general. They were in fact more interested at this time in the characters they had created using the computer program and the actions they had used to animate them.
> **Julie**: Yes, and as they hadn't even met Keyboard yet, they weren't even slightly interested in her reactions.
> **Penny**: We are just very lucky they are a very polite group of children who are willing to wait and re-engage when there is something to connect to . . .

Fortunately, there were successes within this particular lesson as well, including the arrival of Sparky. Here the dramatic tension of surprise was used to great effect, occurring within a sequence where Julie, in role as Keyboard (complete with a colander on her head and iPad attached to her waist), has just arrived to meet the children face-to-face for the first time, and is complaining about her daughter Rollo. By introducing the robot dog at this time, we were looking for ways to maintain the children's engagement and to extend opportunities for language development and interaction. The following vignette reveals more detail about this moment:

The children are engaged in a visit with Keyboard (Rollo's mother), who has arrived from Buttonridge to look for her daughter. She is expressing her anger with Rollo for being irresponsible and is attempting to get the children to agree that taking the family space ship without permission is not appropriate. The children do not appear to share her views, and politely resist her attempts to get them to paint Rollo as naughty. Suddenly, a small robotic barking sound is heard from outside the classroom and immediately there is recognition that this is the moment they have all been waiting for . . . Sparky has arrived. The children rush to the door, but respectfully make a pathway for the battery driven robot dog, complete with wagging tail, to enter the room. There is great excitement, even awe as the dog they have previously only seen in photos sent by email or shared with them by Keyboard, is suddenly 'real' and in their classroom. Katie announces, 'Welcome to ESL2 Sparky'.

The reunion is a joyous one, with the children taking turns to talk to Sparky one on one, asking him questions and generally engaging with him as a long, lost friend now returned. Fortunately, Keyboard is able to translate Sparky's barked answers for them and soon the children have a whole lot of new information about where he has been these past weeks.

Overall, the children's responses indicated both delight and amazement. A year later, one of the children excitedly recalled that moment:

Child: You bring the Sparky and . . . we have touch the Sparky. You click the Sparky and it can talk, or it can do something!

With the dog now found, it was time to steer the drama in a new direction, with this new direction being informed by a number of factors. For example, the classroom teacher was keen for the students to use the internet as a research source, while we wanted to be more culturally sensitive and inclusive in our work. We also hoped to take the drama towards a celebratory and fun conclusion. With these ideas in mind, we devised a new character called Blue Ray and decided that the reason that Rollo had come to Earth with Sparky in the first place was that she was trying to find out about Earth weddings so that she could have an Earth-style wedding when she married her fiancé, Blue Ray.

Rollo told the children that she was once again seeking their help. As 'experts' from many different countries she imagined that they would have significant knowledge about all the different kinds of human wedding ceremonies that happened on Earth. The children responded with rather confused looks on their faces. They didn't know the word wedding. With the help of the classroom teacher, they used the internet (and YouTube in particular) to research about different types of weddings. When we returned to the classroom they had joyfully selected a Bollywood-style wedding for Rollo and Blue Ray!

The drama concluded with the children attending the wedding ceremony as guests. They created their own costumes and messages of goodwill which were formally and quite ceremoniously delivered to the bride and groom.

Throughout the period that we were working in the classroom we sought the teacher's feedback to ensure that we were supporting her programme. She worked extensively with the children between our visits as well to provide further opportunities for the children. At the end of the first series of lessons we interviewed Katie more formally, seeking her feedback about the work we had done. She told us:

> I thought it was a really useful tool for lots of different things. I thought it was really good for their vocab building because of the story. . . . It absolutely, definitely complimented what we do even though we're not learning about outer space and aliens getting married! But it's all part of the holistic vocab building experience.

Yet she also indicated that she had been sceptical at first that the approach would work.

> I was a bit worried at first because they are all new arrivals and they don't have much language. I was wondering how the story would go

and I just kept thinking you guys would have to work so hard to get the responses back but I was really surprised how much they got into the story and how you guys were able to draw the language out as well.

She indicated three reasons that, for her, were central to the success of the work: the fact that it had been fun, that it was someone different from outside their normal classroom interactions coming in to work with them and because it offered an animated experience. Later in the same interview she extended on this idea, stating that it was like the children had developed a relationship with the character. This was supported by a comment from one of the children who we interviewed a year later.

> **Child**: I remember that we make a . . . a poster of Rollo Robot, and Sparky. We make and we put on the computer. We have our own, uh, we have our own video and we have learn many things about robot . . . keyboard . . . Sparky, Rollo, and some of the robots. We have draw about robot, and about we . . . our friend.

Katie also explained how it built on the work that she had been doing with the children:

> **Katie**: I guess they had a bit of knowledge and understanding because our topic was space, so we'd covered a few of those key words and it seemed to build on that and make a bit of sense.

Katie explained how hard it was to find a shared experience that she could draw on when planning her programme with the children and the way that would lead to selecting something quite broad and not necessarily as engaging as a basis. The creation of the drama experience counteracted this, offering a shared experience that was engaging to the children. It allowed her to build on the work we were doing between our visits.

The more language the children had, the more they were able to engage confidently in the work. Those with very limited language struggled at times to follow the narrative and events of the drama.

However, Katie noted that the way that we had structured the work did offer protection for the more reserved or less confident children too.

> **Katie**: But I think the way that you guys did it, not expecting each child to get up and perform something was really good for them because I don't think that they felt under pressure or inadequate in anyway. That was a really good thing.

She also noted that at times she had been surprised to see that the drama had encouraged children who would not normally get up and speak in front of others to do so. For her, the process drama had created opportunities for more reluctant speakers to participate that are not normally available to them. As one of the children told us a year later:

> **Child**: Like, I have never speak at the front of the people before, but you come, you teach us how to do that, and I have done that.

At times, the research team worried that they might only be catering to the needs of the children with higher English language levels, but Katie disagreed. She speculated that the visual nature of the work offered opportunities for all the children and contributed to its success.

> **Katie**: For people who don't have a lot of language . . . because it's drama, it's something they can get from watching you and they're very good at that, picking up all sort of nonverbal cues. I think they got a lot out of it.

Other benefits noted by Katie included the opportunities the drama work gave for children to interact with each other and support each other as they worked. She noted that they normally struggled with group work without an adult to support them but that here they had managed to work in groups without the need for such support.

On reflection, the phase 1 drama work did, on the whole, support the principles outlined earlier. It offered opportunities for the children to learn language in context and with purpose. It offered rich opportunities for expression and interaction. It was able to cater to and support individual learners within the group context. It offered opportunities for the children to develop confidence and saw them willing to take risks. The use of process drama supported their motivation to learn and develop as speakers, readers and writers of English. It also offered the children the opportunity to develop positive relationships with each other and with us.

> **Child**: Because it can make you . . . talk a lot of the . . . thing, like you talk about Sparky, or the Rollo like that, and it make you can talk better or . . . like you say, you have three friend, and one person say, one person do the action like that, and you say, you will know how to do very well.

In terms of the limitations of the work, we also had some ideas, with perhaps the most important of these being the sense that the children missed out on a major aspect of drama work by not being given the opportunity to adopt a role themselves. Our concerns, within both this phase of the project and the earlier pilot work, had been that the language demands of working in role might be too challenging. However, having witnessed the children's commitment to the characters in these two dramas, we were determined that in the next phase we would design a drama that required all participants to work in role – to experience the full power of process drama. As experienced drama educators we knew that the children would be able to exercise far more agency in the drama if they were working from within the dramatic context and that they would be empowered through their roles to contribute to its direction.

Phase 2 – A Magic Man

The following year, Julie and Penny returned to the same classroom to work with Katie and her new class of children. We recognized a few faces from our previous work, but most of the children in the class were new. Although there were again some children with very little English, the language development of most of the children was not as limited as it had been with the previous class.

Katie informed us that her curriculum focus for the term was to be legends. The mandated syllabus required an understanding of legends as a genre of storytelling, with an additional goal being to reinforce the idea that legends were generally passed down in oral form from one generation to the next over many centuries. With the key learning about role also fresh in our minds, we decided to create a drama with two time layers, with the children taking role both as the people of the past involved directly in the events described in the legend and as contemporary historians trying to understand its origins. Clearly this was a complex structure for children with beginner English language skills, but somewhat surprisingly, we weren't daunted.

We decided to use a legend about a wise woman as the pretext for the drama. We both had worked with this pretext before. It is a story about an ancient island community who relied on fishing for their livelihood. One day, following a terrible storm, the fish disappeared. The people of the island went to the wise woman of their island to seek her help. She promised to make the fish return if they met three demands that she placed on them.

In choosing to use this tale with the children, we opted not to share the whole story straight away, but rather to work with just part of it at first, simply introducing the idea that the story was from long, long ago and was about a group of people who lived on an island where all the fish had disappeared following a fierce but mysterious storm. In the first 2 weeks then, the children worked to build belief in this island. They imagined it to have a dark, dark forest, scary caves, a broken mountain (a volcano) and a harbour. They created and took role as the people they imagined to live there. Some chose to adopt generalized roles such as mother, farmer, fisherman, teacher, nurse, doctor, while others chose more specific roles. One boy declared that he was king of the island. Another told us he was Baboo who lived on 'Dark and Scary Cave Island'. A third chose to take role as a mysterious old man called Kocho who lived down by the harbour. Importantly, these roles were not pre-determined by the original legend or even suggested by us as drama facilitators, but were developed by the children themselves as they interacted with each other and us through a range of in-role events.

Between visits, the classroom teacher worked with the children to expand upon the initial ideas developed during our visit. Through a range of writing and drawing tasks the children named the island (somewhat ironically) as the 'Island of Plenty Fish'; developed the original map of the island by naming its key geographic features; and completed a character profile sheet outlining the background, family circumstances and interests of their character.

In the next session the children used movement and vocal work to create the terrible storm that they imagined had occurred. Some enacted trees falling in the forest. They considered other dangers these people may have faced in their lives on the island and took great pleasure in

Figure 6 The map of the island.

creating this dangerous world. One of the strategies that we used to explore their ideas but to keep the space as safe as possible was freeze-frames. As suggestions of the various dangers were offered, the children worked simultaneously in groups to create images representing their characters' responses to these events.

One suggestion that generated a fascinating outcome was that a tsunami might have once threatened these people. This led to a discussion about how the people might have survived, with retreat to the island's caves or the top of the volcano being seen as possible escape routes. However, one group had a different response and offered a very convincing enactment of Baboo from the 'Dark and Scary Cave Island' forcing back the water using his considerable magical powers. With his arms raised to the waters as the other children (as villagers) hid behind him, his face became fierce and determined. The image created was a powerful one and he was immediately renamed as 'Baboo the Magic Man'. Suddenly our drama had a new and very important character, while this child's individual status both in the drama and beyond it had been lifted.

During our next visit, this character and the children's responses to him and his powers would prove to be very significant. The vignette below outlines what happened that day:

We sign in as school visitors before walking the short distance across the playground to the ESL 2 (English as a Second Language – Group 2) classroom. Strains of children singing a folk song can be heard as we lug video cameras, tripods, a variety of teaching resources and drama props upstairs. As we enter the classroom the children are rehearsing a song and dance performance drawn from one of the many cultures represented within the group. They will soon perform this for the whole school. They offer to sing it again for us as their first 'outside' audience. We are delighted by the performance, congratulate them, and begin to ready the children and ourselves for the ninety-minute drama session.

We begin with a sharing of the work completed by the children since our last visit, and are particularly impressed by the extensive work they have done in the area of role development. In addition, they proudly share with us their island map that is now far more detailed. Following this sharing, Penny outlines what will occur in the next part of the drama. Inviting the children to take on their roles once again, she invites them to come together in the village market place to discuss once again their concerns about what might happen to them if the fish do not return. Someone immediately suggests an easy solution. They will simply go to an island nearby and get fish from those people. Responding to their suggestion (and stopping this easy solution), Penny adopts role as a villager from a nearby island and arrives at the meeting. She tells them that she has come to seek their help, telling them that the people of her community also have no fish and that their situation is desperate. The children (in role) look serious as they contemplate the situation and discuss the causes for the disappearance, including that the water has become too hot and that they might have all gone into the Scary Cave.

We are about to introduce, the idea of the wise woman and her demands (via Julie in role as this woman), when the young boy who has adopted the role of Baboo from Scary Island, claims that he can make fish and will give them to the visitor. Penny challenges him by saying that if he had fish, why didn't he give them to his people – she is concerned that this is another easy solution. Another child offers the idea that they should all move to another country, but there is no support for this idea. Suddenly, one of the girls spontaneously offers the creative suggestion that the fish might come back if the people did a slow dance and that if they keep dancing they might be able to make the fish come back. Excited by this idea, one of the children immediately suggests they try it and counts ready 1, 2, 3. Both Penny and the children respond, moving randomly in the space until Penny stops dancing and as the visitor from the nearby island notes that she has heard that the people of this island have some songs and dances that they use on special occasions. The children immediately make the connection to the song and dance they were rehearsing for the school event and become very excited, with individuals organizing others into lines and preparing to dance. Significantly there are distinct differences in the dancing and singing, whilst the children refer to each other by their in-role names and maintain their various characters. For example, Baboo becomes a leader in the dance, while the King chooses not to dance at all, but rather to watch with arms folded. Suddenly Baboo announces in a loud voice, 'I'm hungry' and the dancing stops. Suddenly, the boy playing Kocho, the old man who lives by the harbour, calls out, 'Look, here's a fish!' Suddenly there are fish everywhere and the children excitedly use pieces of paper to represent the fish that have appeared, piling them up into Penny's arms as gifts for the people of her island. Eventually, she calls 'cut' and the action stops.

There is immediate and general laughter as the dramatic world is temporarily suspended to be replaced by discussions out of role about what might happen next, including how the people might be able to sustain this approach to bringing the fish back. They wonder about how tired the people might become if they had to sing and dance all day, and even try out what it might be like to have to sing and dance as they work. Just then, the boy playing the King introduces a new idea to the drama, suggesting that this is how the Magic Man makes the fish – that it is him who is cruelly making the people dance and that he will only bring them fish if they keep dancing. He says: 'We have to give him a fish and then we sing and then he brings us many, many fish! We have to sing many, many times.'

Later, we consider what might eventually have happened to these people. Ideas offered are rich and exciting, including: the idea that the King becomes tired of the threats made by the Magic Man and leads his people away from the island; that the King did not like all this singing, and threatens to turn everyone to stone if they don't leave the island immediately; and even that the volcano begins to erupt, forcing the people to flee to safety by climbing into boats and crossing the water to seek new homes.

During his interview at the conclusion of the project, the boy from the Congo who played the King offered his views on the drama work, suggesting that he likes drama 'because I can learn more things, and I want to learn so much'. This is his summary of what he believes happened on this island:

> Um, it was the island and there were living people good, so all . . . uh, Baboo the magic man get angry, and then he said because he was telling people to sing every day, to sing where they are, they sing, but they stop. And then the King said, you stop to sing now. And then he bring a volcano erupt. And then people run.

The children were keen to explore the options they had come up with in action, but we were unsure. Suddenly the drama felt like it was coming too close to their lived realities – with people fleeing their homes to seek a new life because of terrible danger. Through their agency within the drama work, they were taking us in directions we were keen to avoid. However, from the outset we had determined that we would try to stay true to the principles we had established, including the application of a pedagogy that empowered the learners and gave them opportunities to exercise agency. We therefore invited the children to explore these journeys of departure, feeling somewhat concerned as they did:

> As the children enact their journey across the sea, with the child playing the King standing in the boat shouting orders and children struggling to paddle hard to escape the impending volcano, Penny and I look at each other. In spite of our best intentions, the children are now in role as boat people, escaping from their homelands. We smile somewhat ironically. All our best efforts at distancing had brought us here. What we witnessed however was nothing to concern us. The children were enjoying the exploration of these people's fate, with the connections made apparently being ours – not theirs.

After this session we met as a planning team and decided it was time to move on, to explore the ideas in the outer layer of this narrative. With this in mind, Julie took role as a representative of the History Channel, who was seeking 'experts' to make a documentary about the Island of Plenty Fish. She addressed the children as experts, telling them that the island was now abandoned and that she had funding to make a documentary about what had happened so long ago to make all the people disappear.

The children were given the task of applying for a job at the History Channel. They completed a written job application and each was interviewed by the Professor, with everyone observing as others were interviewed. These interactions became more and more playful as the children told the Professor what they were good at and how much money they expected to earn.

Once all the children had been employed by the History Channel, Julie showed them a shawl she was carrying and indicated that she would wear it to indicate her role as a very old woman whose family had passed on to her information about what had actually happened to the people of Plenty Fish Island. This information had been passed down to her through her family. Julie was about to adopt this role when one of the children took control of the action:

Julie is about to step into the hot seat as the old woman when a young boy jumps to his feet and asks if he can play the role. We immediately agree, but are surprised by his enthusiasm and the agency he is showing in making this request. A normally very shy and quiet boy, he suddenly seems different – empowered. Then, and once again to our surprise, he runs to the front of the classroom and fetches a timber window opener with a hook on its end and indicates that he will use it as a walking stick to further support his role as the old woman. He is animated and excited as he takes the hot seat 'becoming' the old woman to answer the questions of the other children who are in role as the historians. With limited language, he nevertheless manages to communicate the story he so clearly was imagining in his head. Given our perception (and that of the teacher) of him as a shy boy from a culture less inclined to performance than the African children in the class who appeared to be more natural story tellers, we see this as a moment to savour – especially as several other children immediately follow his lead, asking if they too can have a go at putting on the shawl and becoming the old woman.

Within interviews conducted following the drama work, this child outlined his previous experiences of learning English:

I was in my country you have to speak English, I little bit English . . . and you not speak English, she hit you with stick. In my country, you have to speak English, because in my country some people don't know English. Me too . . . just a little bit English. And I came here, just I say, 'Hallo' or something like that.

Katie also commented on his contributions that day when she noted:

(This child) sticks out you know . . . he was really into it. And he's one of the children who has very limited English, but that was his comfort zone, you know. So that was really good, I thought that day was really, really good.

In later sessions the children built on their roles as historians by working in groups to make films about the legend of Plenty Fish Island. With some working as camera operators, using iPads to capture the action, others re-enacted their ideas about what might have happened to the people of this island. We had expected that this section of the overall drama experience would be highly engaging and that the children would appreciate the opportunity to work with the technology. However, our expectations were not met, as the children's engagement with this task was nowhere near as high as we had anticipated. It seemed to us that they were far more interested in living the legend than recreating it, and that rather than enhancing their learning, the technology at this time hindered it. The drama lurched to an unconvincing conclusion.

At the conclusion of our work with the children, we once again interviewed Katie about her perceptions. We were particularly interested in her comments about the children's participation and her thoughts about whether or not the drama had catered to the needs of children with different levels of language acquisition and of differing abilities.

> **Katie**: I think what it does is it allows all of the children to participate, but at the level they are comfortable with, you know, I mean in terms of their language, not necessarily their self-confidence, you know. So the people whose English is at a higher level, they can obviously contribute a lot more, but those that can't, who have limited English, they can still join in, they can do actions, or give one-word responses, so you don't have to have English that's a certain level to be able to get something out of it. So I like that because it scaffolds all the children.

Later in the same interview this was further illustrated when she spoke about one of the boys who had made a significant contribution to the drama and had been very engaged in the work:

> **Katie**: for him, I think, it's a great opportunity to just get in there and play, and have some fun and . . . get a bit of success, because you know, in the classroom, academically, he struggles, . . . and there aren't too many . . . he's not very good at sports, he's had lots of incidents, always lots of dramas with the other kids, so there's not much success, full stop. But at least in drama, he can be . . . you know, he can have a role, and he can succeed.

She confirmed that the drama had also supported her teaching programme more generally, with the children learning not only new vocabulary but also new concepts that could be transferred to other areas of the curriculum.

Katie Yes, well, I think it's a good context for them. So you know, you come in and you create a story . . . and you know lots of new language is learnt, so they learn lots of vocabulary, and lots of new concepts, and interestingly, you can see it transfer across to other learning areas, because in SOSE (Studies of Society and the Environment) we've been looking at different environments and I hadn't planned to talk about islands, but they were keen, so we looked at lots of different islands in Australia. So you know, you can see, it's provided a good basis for them – for us – to build on it. And I can see lots of the language coming out, and the concepts, you know. They seem to think all islands have volcanoes (laughs). And dead fish! And watch out for the storms! You know, but you can see it. They were doing some creative writing last week, and they had to choose one environment that they would like to live in, and give me a reason why. And they all except for two, wrote about islands, but I know it was because they knew more, they were able to express their ideas. So it wasn't necessarily that they all wanted to live on an island, but they'd been given that language to use, and you could see it in their writing as well. So I thought that was interesting.

Similar to her response the previous year, Katie also felt that the second process drama (which was quite different to the first one) offered opportunities for interaction among the children that did not always happen in other lessons in the classroom.

Katie: I think that day we had them sitting in the circle, and they were working in groups, and they had to act out a scene or something. . . . I thought they all did really well working with each other, because they were in very mixed ability groups, and they had to talk to themselves – talk amongst themselves, to work out what was going to happen. And I know we helped them, but it was great to see them all working together, you know, all the different levels of English.

As well, the work was perceived to be fun, with the children enthusiastically engaging.

> **Katie**: And I think that's to do with the teaching styles they've been exposed to. It's very rote. See that's another benefit of drama, you know. For a lot of these children, they've come from a very . . . you know, it's a very strict environment and it's all just copying from the board. It's reading and writing and arithmetic and that's it, so, it's a good opportunity for them to do something that's fun.

A good indication that the children were engaged and enjoying the drama work occurred with this group after only one lesson. One young girl asked if we would come back the next day. We said no, they had other work to do with their teacher too. She then eagerly suggested that everybody come to school on the weekend to work with us as they didn't have to do other schoolwork then!

Katie also confirmed that the work that we had done supported her own teaching and learning programme, with the fictional story created forming the basis for further language activities.

> **Katie**: We did with the map, and we did a writing activity where they had to write down what their typical day looked like, and what did they remember about growing up on the island. And we got some responses from that, you know, like 'I would go fishing with my friends', or 'we would play on the island', or 'I would go to . . .' whoever their friend's character was.

In summing up the advantages of the process drama approach we had used, Katie stated:

> **Katie**: Opportunities to talk. . . . Well, I think it provides a sort of a safe zone where they can use whatever language they have, and it's . . . I see it, as the teacher, as being the time where you're not sort of saying, 'This is how you pronounce it' or teaching language. It's about them, being able to express their ideas at their level, you know, whatever language works. If it's a one-word answer, for me,

if it's a trying to find the right words and we help them in that area, that's great! I think it has to be . . . you have to have some activities, for the children, where they're able to communicate in their own words. It can't always be about learning language, you got to be able to just enjoy it and use it.

She later added:

> **Katie**: Because I think it would be very hard, to constantly be thinking of those words, the right words, the right context, and to be able to express it, it's got to be very tiring for them, very hard, so they've got to really want to get their ideas across, and I think in drama they can do that. You know, it's interesting, it's fun, so . . . for the children, they do that.

One young boy in the class told us that he thought drama was a good way to learn. When asked why he thought this, he stated:

> **Child**: Because you can know more things, and then you can say more things.

What was achieved and how well did the project respond to its guiding principles?

The material outlined above has provided key insights into the work completed across the three phases of the project. We learnt about working with children from refugee backgrounds, about working as language educators in beginner language classrooms, about the possibilities and limitations of using drama pedagogies in this context and about the importance of partnerships. We also learnt more about our philosophical principles and as such this section is arranged once again according to these. Here we will draw on this material to identify the strengths and weaknesses of our approach, using the guiding principles offered earlier in the chapter as a framework.

Valuing each child as an individual

The children involved in this project were indeed highly individual, with this individuality being revealed in many different ways. For example, while the material above reveals that some of the children were clearly confident enough in their participation to take agency in the drama, offering ideas and actions to shift the various narratives and redirect them through their participation, others were more comfortable in adopting passive roles that allowed them to simply follow the existing narrative. As illustrated in the descriptions of the drama and in the teacher's comments above, these degrees of willingness were not necessarily aligned to academic ability, with children who struggled academically sometimes being the ones to take the lead in the drama work.

Cultural differences were less of a factor than we had anticipated, with individuals from all cultures responding in their own unique ways, sometimes even surprising us. Here the case of the boy who so keenly embraced the individual role of the old woman was a strong example.

The drama work offered opportunities for both girls and boys to equally participate. Although some of the boys were more vocal and therefore had the potential to dominate in the dramas, there were individual girls who took the lead as well. For instance, in phase 2, both the suggestion to dance and the initiation of the dancing had come from one of the girls in the group.

The drama work catered for individuality and ensured that each child was able to participate at the level they were able to. As Katie noted:

> I think it is, because it's, once again, it's something that you can provide that doesn't rely on having very good literacy skills. You don't *have* to be able to read and write at a certain level to participate in drama, but you *do* need to be able to read and write to do a lot of things when you start getting into upper primary. You have to have those skills, and if you don't you struggle in Science, you struggle in SOSE, you struggle in Maths, you know, you *struggle*. And I think in drama, you know,

it takes that away. I mean yes, you do use literacy skills or you need literacy skills, but you can also get by, and get some success just by participating and having a go.

Safe spaces

The descriptions offered above also highlight that it is possible to structure drama work that is imaginative and engaging and that does not rely on, refer to or deal with trauma stories. Interestingly, however, while the dramatic worlds created by and within the drama work were focused on tall tales and legends, placing them far beyond approaches that begin with trauma, stories of home or even arrival stories, connections to the children's lived experiences nevertheless emerged. These connections provided the children with opportunities to respond empathically to characters in crisis, offering them support, encouragement and ways of coping.

These experiences were not traumatic however, for as Katie noted:

> it (drama) provides a good safe space, doesn't it, to explore and play. . . . But I think, you know, the level of enjoyment is really evident, isn't it? On their faces, you know, the way they are bouncing around, and (laughs) . . . I mean I don't think that it touched on anything traumatic or brought up anything that was unresolved or had happened to them or anything like that. I didn't see any evidence of that. I saw just a lot of enjoyment and . . . but also you could see how it *might* provide . . . if you wanted to go there, if you wanted to explore things, or perhaps a counsellor, I mean it'd be a good way of touching on things, wouldn't it, and finding out, you know, what's actually going on in their heads.

In her final comments here she was clearly suggesting that she saw scope for process drama to be used within a counselling context to enable the children to safely explore trauma stories. Such an approach, though, needs to be handled with particular care and requires a partnership approach with a trained counsellor.

Language as a key aspect of resilience

When asked about the value of the work, Katie had no hesitation when she responded:

> What the children get out of it. Definitely. The learning, from a language perspective, and a literacy perspective, but also their confidence, you know, their self-esteem, their self confidence, just having that free area that zone to talk and communicate without having . . . without feeling self conscious about their language and cooperating with peers.

In the work that we did with these children, opportunities to develop some of the key skills associated with resilience were present. The approach motivated the children to learn. The risk-free environment of the drama provided them with opportunities to speak with confidence. Their writing improved. They had opportunities to use language in meaningful ways and with purpose. They felt a sense of success through their engagement and individual achievements. The work we did together also offered opportunities for all of us to develop positive adult–child relationships.

One aspect that we noted in particular was the way the fictional world created in the classroom provided a rich, shared context for the children and teachers to build on further. The richness of the context relates to the imaginative context created and explored and also to the way engagement in drama occurs. Dramatic engagement involves an intellectual, a physical and an emotional response. As was noted by the teacher earlier, the work offered the children an opportunity for an animated response.

Empowering pedagogies

Our own observations and those of the classroom teacher support the notion that the children felt empowered within the work. They engaged enthusiastically and eagerly looked forward to our return visits. Their willingness to offer suggestions for new directions in the narrative of the drama indicated the agency they felt as they worked. Providing opportunities for children to assume fictional roles that have higher status than the roles of the adults with whom they are interacting further encourages this.

As a pedagogical approach, process drama offered opportunities for children with different levels of language ability and with different social skills and desired ways of interacting with others, the possibility of engaging meaningfully in the work. As Katie stated:

> It's a great experience for the students. They get a lot of out it in terms of their language, but it also provides a good starting point for you as a teacher. You know, you can take it and run with it in whatever direction you want to. So if you want to focus on the oral language, you know get them to, you know, to get them to talk about it, or pretend to be somebody, or to tell another student or another class about it. You know you could focus on that, you could focus on the writing side, we could focus on the technology. So you as a teacher can often take it on a different strand, but I think really, it's about them, it's about what *they* get out of it.

The work offered a shared and engaging experience with an appropriate balance of challenge and protection. As such, it was able to cater to the diverse needs of the children in the classes in which we worked. Those who preferred to work in a more reserved or quiet way were as engaged as others who verbalized their responses more freely. The children did not feel pressure to respond in a particular way.

The process drama experiences also extended the opportunities that the children had to interact with each other and enhanced their abilities to work together in peer groups without close adult support and direction. Further advantages of our approach included opportunities to build relationships with others in new and different ways. This included building relationships with other children, with a range of adults and also building relationships with fictional characters.

The classroom teacher referred to the drama as a safe zone. It offered the children opportunities to feel successful and through this they developed confidence and a willingness to take further risks.

The process drama approach adopted involved a number of strategies that were useful in this context including teacher-in-role, writing-in-role, freeze-frames, movement and role development and interaction. In addition, by following the children's lead and giving them opportunities to direct the action of the drama, we were being true to the style of work valued by drama educators in other learning contexts who work with a range of different participant groups.

Reciprocal learning through a strong partnership

Without a doubt, a key ingredient for success within this project was the strong partnership we developed with the school staff, and in particular the teachers and assistant teachers we worked with. Not only did they participate enthusiastically with us in the lessons, but they also did extensive follow-up and preparation work with the children between our visits. Without this mutual commitment and involvement, it is unlikely that the children would have had such rich and engaging experiences. It is also unlikely that we would have learnt as much as *we* did about the use of process drama in a context like this. Across the three phases of the project then, a good deal of reciprocal learning occurred, with our team gaining valuable insights into our practices, especially pedagogical and planning practices.

Our first major learning was about planning at the macro level. Macro-level planning in drama (Dunn and Stinson 2012) refers to the planning that takes place prior to entering the teaching and learning context. It includes the selection or creation of the pretext that will drive the work and the strategies that might be most effectively applied in realizing the development of a dramatic world built upon that material. Here we discovered that we had been too concerned with distancing, being extremely careful in selecting material that would ensure that the children were not adversely affected or even traumatized. Our experiences showed us, however, that we should have placed greater trust in the form, that through the use of a fictional context, all kinds of ideas can be explored in a safe and engaging manner, while nonetheless tapping into key emotions like sympathy and empathy.

This is evident across all three phases of the project. For example, within the pilot study, a fantasy context involving a giant was chosen. Here we hoped that the use of this commonly explored fictional topic would ensure that the drama work offered a safe experience. However, it was clear that within this work the children were identifying deeply with the plight of the giant, understanding in a highly intuitive way the reasons why he might be angry.

Again, in the Island of Plenty Fish drama there were moments when we had worried that the work might become traumatic or too close to their personal experiences. In hindsight, it was evident that the children relished the moments that they themselves had suggested we create.

Across all three phases we also learnt a good deal about the potential affordances of digital technologies within process drama work focused on language learning. In particular, we found that these technologies could prove themselves to be highly useful as a way of extending, reinforcing and reviewing language, supporting the children's narrative skills, enhancing the mood of the drama and offering opportunities for the children to exercise agency (Dunn et al. 2012). However, we also learnt that their integration into the work was most successful when they were carefully introduced through scaffolded learning experiences. They were of less value when this did not occur and there was less of a link between their use and the narrative being developed.

Finally, although most children valued the approach and felt that it helped them with their speaking and writing, a couple of the children found that at times it made writing tasks more frustrating. They expressed the view that while they had a stronger desire to communicate their ideas and clear reasons to do this, they lacked the necessary written English skills to record what they wanted to communicate.

Challenges

The work has also thrown up challenges and areas that are in need of further research. One of the most important of these is that of sustainability, with questions arising for us about what our work has left behind. While working alongside us, the classroom teacher undoubtedly built knowledge and skills about our approach. However, she also mentioned that she would find it difficult to use some of the strategies that we were using. Furthermore, we wondered how, given the tight time, space and curriculum constraints, we might have empowered a greater number of teachers from this school community and beyond, to use this pedagogical approach.

We also wondered what might have happened had the teacher we worked with not been so enthusiastic and willing to take risks. No doubt the quality of the work would have been significantly reduced had she been reluctant to participate or if she had a different philosophy than us. Given the fact that the mandated curriculum and testing demands of education authorities have the potential to limit the time that teachers might be prepared to adopt an approach as time consuming as process drama, we saw this as an additional challenge. Perhaps, unlike the principal and staff we worked with, they might believe that better test scores might be achieved if a more conservative or traditional learning approach were to be used.

Finally, the parent involvement within this project was minimal, as the work was process based and didn't result in a grand performance or display and we wondered what might have been achieved had parents been given the chance to be more involved in our work. Fortunately, we did hear from some of the children, via their interviews with us, that they themselves had kept their parents in the loop about the project, reporting on the events of the drama as they unfolded. However, the learning that occurred in the classroom context was never formally shared with parents or guardians and its outcomes were not publically celebrated.

The future

At the outset of this primary school project our overall goal had been to 'value add' to the settlement process of newly arrived refugee children. Across this chapter we have reported in detail on our experiences as drama educators working in partnership with two classroom teachers and a school administration team willing to allow us the time to explore what might be achieved in this regard by applying the structures and strategies of process drama. Our report here reveals that we had both successes and failures, but that overall it was a highly positive experience for all involved. In the absence of statistics or 'hard data' to 'prove' our effectiveness, we may never be able to convince those in policy positions that process drama is an effective pedagogy to support this settlement process. Further studies that adopt a mixed-method approach are therefore needed – studies that will hopefully enable us to capture in numerical form what these experiences have so powerfully revealed – that drama is an empowering and engaging pedagogy that does indeed offer children new ways to see themselves as learners and members of their new community.

5

Acting Against Bullying: Managing Conflict and Bullying in a Secondary Drama Classroom

We noticed that Ali was very late for the first workshop in week eight of the project. This was most unusual, because this sixteen-year-old Sudanese boy who had recently arrived in Australia was one of the most enthusiastic students in the Acting Against Bullying classes run as one of the projects included in this overarching resettlement project. When he did arrive, Ali slipped quietly into the back of the room, and then joined a group of African boys who were working on a drama about physical bullying. One of the research team reported that Ali's clothes were torn and there was blood on his trousers. I drew him aside and asked what had happened. He claimed he had fallen over and injured himself and 'it was all fixed up.'

However, whilst watching the group dramas about bullying, we were alerted by Ali's intense involvement in the scenario where he played the role of a victim being attacked by a group of bullies. Jenny (the class teacher) spoke to him privately, and Ali revealed that he had been attacked at the railway station by a gang of young men. These Sudanese youths were trying to make Ali join their gang, and they had harassed him on a number of occasions. We asked Ali what he wanted to do about it, and he said that tomorrow he would bring his machete with him on the train and use it on the gang.

Jenny and I attempted to discuss the situation with him to help him find a solution that did not involve violence, but he was too distressed to consider other options. We then suggested he see the school counsellor, but he refused, indicating that he did not trust authority figures. However, he did agree to return to the drama and try out a range of solutions to his real problem by fictionalizing it and acting out different possibilities. He did so, not in role as the victim of physical bullying, but as the director of the drama, with one of the student researchers taking on the role of the young person being bullied. As a result of this experience, Ali decided that he actually needed help to resolve the bullying, and went with the teacher to the counsellor. The school and the community police officers provided him with that support, and the bullying ceased altogether. As well, Ali spoke to a number of members of the gang individually to explain why he was so committed to continuing his schooling and why he had no intention of joining them.

In an interview at the end of the project, Ali was asked what he had learnt from the Acting Against Bullying Project:

> Ali: I solve it like . . . it's helped like how to solve bullying . . . how to get away from bullying. Sometimes when someone wants to fight me or someone wants to do anything to me, I know to get away from him how to confuse him, not to make him get angry so much. I know how to treat people too and things that it is not good to be cool. Sometimes I realize that if I do this to this person, he will gets angry and then I will realize that I'm not going to do it, 'cos if I do it he will get angry, so what I do, I am not going to do it, I am going to do things that he will be happy and appreciate.

Ali was just one of the 32 newly arrived teenagers from a refugee background who participated in the Acting Against Bullying Project discussed in this chapter. Jenny (all names used are pseudonyms), the classroom teacher in the language unit, and Arisa, the refugee co-ordinator at the school, both requested that this project be used with their adolescent students, believing that being able to manage conflict and bullying was an essential part of the settlement process. Both Jenny and Arisa had previously heard about the Acting Against Bullying programme and were aware of publications outlining its success as a bullying management programme for schools. They were also aware that the programme uses drama techniques and Enhanced Forum Theatre (see Chapter 3) to explore and address issues of conflict and bullying in schools, followed by a later phase where the students teach these concepts to other children. These teachers hoped that this approach would be equally successful with new arrivals.

For newly arrived refugees in schools, bullying is a particular issue because they are often ill-equipped to deal with it. Correa-Velez et al. (2010) note that: 'Previous research has identified bullying as one of the key problems refugee youth experience at school' (p. 1406). Onsando and Billett (2009) found that African students studying in technical institutes in Australia suffered from both racial discrimination and social exclusion. 'The effects of racial discrimination extended to the participants' feelings of being isolated and stereotyped as inferior beings' (84). In their Canadian survey of the resettlement experiences of immigrant and refugee youth, Rossiter and Rossiter (2009) found: 'In addition to academic, cultural and linguistic barriers, participants perceived bullying to be problem for immigrant and refugee youth in many schools, particularly verbal bullying, name-calling and teasing' (p. 418).

Having discussed their request with Jenny and Arisa, we visited the English Language Unit to meet the students, and as a result we agreed that the Acting Against Bullying programme could be valuable in providing them with the understanding and techniques to deal with conflict and bullying issues both now and in the future, as it had done with students of all ages in mainstream schools in a number of different countries. Acting Against Bullying (Burton and O'Toole 2009) involves teaching students about bullying, using drama techniques to explore and address issues of conflict and bullying in schools, and then encouraging the students to teach other children so they learn from each other. When we spoke to them, the new arrivals at Riverside High School expressed a lively interest in learning how to deal with conflict and bullying through drama, and we were encouraged by their enthusiasm. We also hoped that the programme would enhance their spoken language and their sense of identity and confidence as it had done for many students in mainstream schools.

Working in a team that included these teachers and their students, project team member Bruce Burton, Nadia Vanek, a graduate applied theatre researcher, and up to five final year students of a Bachelor of Arts in Applied Theatre programme who acted as research assistants on work integrated learning placements, the Acting Against Bullying workshops were conducted three times a week for 5 months, with each session being of 90-minutes duration.

The participants

The young participants involved in this project were all students of the English Language Unit that had been established in this large high school to cater for the significant population of newly arrived students, including those with refugee status and others who were immigrants. The school is innovative and proactive in providing an education for these young people, and the teachers are particularly dedicated and effective in teaching students of different cultures, languages and family backgrounds. As a result, the atmosphere in the school is positive, and the majority of the students appear to have warm relationships with the staff. Most seem to enjoy their schooling.

The English Language Unit provides a base and a starting point for the newly arrived young people, offering them instruction in a range of school subjects, including the arts and skills such as computing as well as English. The unit is on the school grounds, but separate from the other buildings with a wire fence around it. This fence was erected because of instances of conflict and bullying between new arrivals and other students. In spite of this situation, students from the language unit also attend classes in the main part of the school, with the Acting Against Bullying Project work taking place in the school's main drama room.

Ranging in age from 14 to 17, the students we worked with in the unit were attempting to adapt not only to schooling but also to the wider society in Australia. The majority were from African nations, but there were also seven participants from Burma. As well, there were individual teenagers from Thailand, Cambodia and China. Many of the students in the language unit had been in refugee camps in a third country for a number of years before arriving in Australia.

Approach

As with the other case studies in the book, the team working on this secondary school project made a conscious decision not to treat the participants as people suffering from dysfunction or trauma, but as lively teenagers interested in learning how to manage conflict and bullying in their lives here and now. We hoped that they would respond in a similar way to the thousands of other young people who have experienced the Acting Against Bullying programme and that they would engage with its drama-based approaches. Our optimism was inspired by the work of Matthews (2008) and Kana and Aitkin (2007) whose arts-based projects had generated high levels of optimism and engagement, together with that of Correa-Velez et al. (2010, p. 1406) whose exploration of the characteristics of young people arriving in Australia noted that they generally have 'high levels of well-being' and are 'well-placed to thrive'.

Of course, from the outset we also understood that we would have to make modifications to the standard Acting Against Bullying approach in order to cater for the specific needs of this diverse group of newly arrived young people and quickly discovered that an extensive range of additional approaches and techniques were required. Many of these additional approaches emerged as a result of the advice offered by the students, their mentors and teachers. Across this process, it also became clear that the students were learning a lot more than how to manage conflict and bullying. They were also developing their socialization skills, gaining a keener critical awareness of their sense of identity and how it is shaped, acquiring new vocabulary and generally developing other language skills including intercultural awareness.

Three action research cycles were implemented by the team during the 5 months of working with the participants. The first cycle involved classroom teaching about the causes and nature of bullying and conflict, and introduced the students to improvised drama as a way of exploring conflict and bullying experiences in different situations from the viewpoints of different people. During this cycle we realized that we needed to encourage language development and cross-cultural and cross-gender socialization if the programme was to work as it had in other schools.

The second cycle involved extensive group activities investigating a range of conflict and bullying scenarios through the use of Enhanced Forum Theatre, an adaptation of Augusto Boal's Theatre of the Oppressed (ref) specifically developed for the Acting Against Bullying programme. Some of the scenarios were fictional, but others drew on the participants' own experiences of settlement, and in a few instances they chose to revisit their experiences as children in their home countries. In this phase the groups were often composed of both girls and boys from different cultural backgrounds. The final cycle focused on the planning and delivery of peer teaching about bullying and conflict to another class in the school.

Rationale

The refugee resettlement literature notes that the preparation young people are given for settlement in Australia and elsewhere is crucial for an effective transition to their new environment. For example, Correa-Valez et al. (2010, p. 1400) argue that 'there is mounting evidence that the resettlement context can have equal if not greater negative impact on well-being as the pre-migration context'. In addition, a number of studies of refugee settlement in different countries have identified the importance of the whole school environment in the process of resettlement (Taylor 2008; Matthews 2008), including the importance of providing a safe and nurturing environment.

In spite of these findings, the nature and number of interventions in settlement experience are often inadequate, and do not provide refugee adolescents with the learning and skills they need. For example, the 32 teenagers we worked with were given just 1 year in the language unit to develop their language skills, adapt to new learning structures and acquire socialization skills, before being placed in standard classes the following year. This is despite the fact that Ferjoa and Vickers (2010, p. 150) note that:

> Existing research has found that four terms of attendance at Intensive English Centres in standard high schools is insufficient to prepare many refugee students for a successful transition to mainstream classrooms. This transition is difficult for students in terms of their learning and acculturation needs, as well as for many of their teachers.

With these ideas in mind, we determined that drama-based approaches might be effective in supporting these multiple settlement demands by providing a safe environment for learning while offering an approach that was language and culture rich. Bolton and Heathcote (1998) argue that all adolescents behave in certain ways based on their personal and cultural belief systems, and classroom drama makes it possible for them to explore and change both beliefs and behaviour. More specifically, Neelands (2009) argues that through drama young people can be led to imagine and look for new ways of living together rather than against each other, to find a shared understanding and to create new models of pluralist community.

In identifying our approach, we drew on the international literature that argues that classroom drama is particularly effective in allowing adolescents to experiment with forms of behaviour and also to transform the way they behave (Burton 1991; O'Neill 1995; Dunn and Anderson 2013). In the drama classroom, students can enact realistic events and characters that can be manipulated and reflected upon, and issues of relationships are dealt with in a safe, fictional context (Morrison et al. 2006). In this way, the participants are both actors and audience, able to experience fictional roles and situations, while perceiving and reflecting on the meaning of these experiences at the same time. The results of Acting Against Bullying programmes previously conducted consistently indicate that secondary school students themselves prefer the use of drama strategies when learning about real-world problems such as bullying in comparison with other forms of instruction (O'Toole et al. 2005).

Perhaps this is because drama provides a safe space for participants to explore issues of culture, society and conflict, and as Hunter (2008, p. 8) asserts: 'The cultivation of a safe space might well be considered an important precursor to any collaborative activity.' Nicholson concurs and argues that drama spaces need to become 'seedbeds of Cultural activity' (2006, p. 15). The safe space provided by drama to experiment with experiences and explore identity is precisely one of the safe and nurturing educational environments that Matthews (2008) identifies as essential to a positive settlement experience. In their project using process drama to explore issues of social exclusion, Kana and Aitkin found that: 'The safety and distance provided by the frame of drama spurred (these) students to grow into positions of leadership in the imagined situation and stand up for issues of social justice for these children' (2007, p. 697).

Acting Against Bullying – Background

The Acting Against Bullying programme is the result of 15 years of action research into conflict and bullying in schools. It began as the international DRACON (a conflation of two words 'drama' and 'conflict') research programme into conflict within schools, with partners in Sweden, Malaysia and Australia (Lofgren and Malm 2005). The programme uses a combination of improvisation, process drama,

Forum theatre and peer teaching, and has evolved into an effective whole school programme that impacts positively on conflict and bullying in both secondary and primary schools. This is particularly significant because bullying remains a serious behavioural problem encountered in schools worldwide.

The key drama strategy in the Acting Against Bullying programme is Enhanced Forum Theatre. Enhanced Forum Theatre allows participants to create and then explore a range of bullying situations, experimenting with strategies and solutions to the problem. As described in Chapter 3, Enhanced Forum Theatre involves the creation of a realistic play in three scenes with each of the scenes depicting one of the three stages of bullying (latent, emerging and manifest). A further requirement of this approach is that each of the scenes also incorporates the three parties involved in bullying (bully, bullied and bystander).

A crucial part of this process is the discussions between the performers and the audience that occur. The first happens when characters are withdrawn from the improvisation and questioned by the audience using the strategy of hot seating. The second is when someone intervenes in the improvisation with a suggestion for change and the whole group engage in discussion about the effectiveness of this intervention. These discussions often last far longer than the actual forum performance, and can generate both creative and practical options for individuals to apply within complex bullying situations.

The other element of the Acting Against Bullying programme that has made it so successful is the use of peer teaching. Extensive research over the past two decades has identified peer teaching as a particularly potent approach to stimulating learning in schools (Goodlad and Hirst 1989; Rubin and Herbert 1998; Gordon 2005). These studies suggest that having students teach, tutor or mentor each other can be an extremely effective means of improving learning in the classroom.

Goodlad and Hirst (1989) identify the positive impact that peer teaching has on student self-esteem, particularly for the students acting as teachers. The range of specific benefits for students doing the peer teaching are described by Rubin and Herbert (1998) as: an increase in social and intellectual awareness; significant gains in empathy; the clear recognition that students could change habitual patterns of behaviour; and finally, that peer teaching empowers students, increasing their sense of mastery and self-esteem. They conclude that it would be hard to think of another method that would enable so much intellectual, social and personal growth. However, as we will discuss later in this chapter, this phase of the Acting Against Bullying process proved to be challenging within the project context.

The research approach

We chose action research as our methodology because the aim of our work was to empower the young people we were working with to manage the conflict and bullying situations they encountered. Action research aims to provide workable solutions to immediate concerns, and to develop human capacities (Kemmis and McTaggart 2008). This is achieved through the process of cycles of action which involve planning, implementing and evaluating strategies and experiences. We decided to use participatory action research because this involves researchers and participants actively collaborating throughout to find solutions to problems (Choudry 2010). The students in the language unit were able to provide practical knowledge drawn from their own experiences of conflict and bullying, while our research team contributed theoretical knowledge and successful strategies to explore effective management. In this way we were able to work together to develop an understanding of a range of conflict and bullying issues relevant to the students and then cooperate to find solutions that they could use in their everyday lives.

As part of their introduction to the project, we told the 32 students about the Acting Against Bullying programme and invited them to participate in the action research as co-researchers. We also asked for their help in obtaining written permission from their parents and guardians if they wished to be involved (all the students did). Preliminary questionnaires were completed by them to provide baseline data about their knowledge and experiences of bullying. A final questionnaire was completed at the end of the project. Jenny, the classroom teacher, took on the responsibility of making sure all the students understood the questionnaires, and devoted an extensive amount of class time to explaining and answering questions about them. The first questionnaire provided us with some useful information about the students' understanding of bullying, and also whether they were currently involved in any way. The final questionnaire sought information about possible changes in their understanding and behaviours as a result of the project. All the workshops were filmed, and detailed observation notes were kept by the members of the research team and by the teachers involved. In other research contexts using this approach, students have been invited to keep reflective journals which are shared with the research team. This was less likely to be successful in this context due to a lack of written English language skills. However, extensive group and individual interviews were conducted throughout the project as an essential element of the participatory action research. These interviews were invaluable in providing us with insights into the impact of the programme on the individual students, and a selection of their comments are offered in this chapter.

Phase 1: Playing, acting, learning

Most of the students had arrived in Australia during the past year and had been at the school for less than 6 months. The majority had studied drama as a subject for the first time during this first semester of schooling in Australia, and none of them had any experience in performance. Furthermore, almost half the 32 students had only begun to learn English in the 6 months before the project began. At the beginning of the programme the seven new arrivals from Burma, together with the Thai and Cambodian boys, struggled to understand even simple instructions and were very reluctant to answer questions, or indeed, speak at all. The African students were much more fluent in English however, but for some of them it was their third spoken language after Swahili and French.

To engage the students initially and encourage them to take on roles and become involved in fictional situations, we introduced a number of drama games and activities. These generated high levels of excitement and involvement, together with a desire to express ideas effectively in English. For example, one of the Thai girls asked for help from one of the student facilitators in pronouncing the words she needed, rehearsing the pronunciation a number of times because she was determined to get it right. As Schewe (2002) observes, drama is a very effective tool in second language learning because in role work the students have the opportunity and confidence to play with different words and sentences, and performance gives them the chance to rehearse and improve their use of language and expression.

As their engagement within this first phase intensified, we increasingly challenged the students with a range of drama activities and exercises, including freeze-frames, mime, spontaneous improvisation and dramatic storytelling. At this stage, we did not focus on conflict or bullying, but instead encouraged the students to explore, as the contexts of their scenarios, their own recent experiences of settlement, schooling, family and friendships, as well as fictional and fantasy stories. We did not explicitly refer to their previous lives or refugee stories, but neither was it specifically excluded. As a result, while individual students occasionally referenced their childhood in these dramas, most of the scenarios were firmly based in the present.

Initially the students chose to work in their ethnic groups, while members of the research team acted as facilitators for each group, providing instructions and advice and modelling the drama techniques being learnt. The level of engagement and enthusiasm was extremely high in this improvised group work, but when we asked the groups to share some of their improvisations in an early workshop, a number of them were reluctant to do so, and despite assistance and encouragement from their facilitators, the performances were very brief, sometimes only a matter of seconds in length.

Despite their reluctance to perform in front of their peers, for those improvised dramas where there was no audience, the students demonstrated impressive developments in their understanding of drama and their skill in using it. We therefore decided to introduce the students to some of the complex concepts and techniques that are fundamental to drama. This approach proved to be effective, not only in developing drama skills, but also in enhancing conceptual understanding and language use. For example, we explicitly taught the concept of transformation, by encouraging the students to transform chairs, lengths of material and their own bodies to create entire contexts for a range of dramas.

The transformation workshop began with the students individually using chairs to represent different kinds of seats of their own choice. They were encouraged to use effective movement and body language to clearly show the nature of the seat. Some pretended they were sitting on seats in cars or buses, while others used the chairs as thrones or toilets. We then asked them to transform the chair into any object of their choice and use it for its purpose, again focusing on their physical movement to make the transformation work. The choices were varied, and ranged from lawn mowers to hats. Some of the male children chose to transform the chairs into weapons of various kinds, which does not normally happen in this workshop with mainstream drama classes or actors in training.

The students used lengths of coloured cloths to create different environments, using blue cloths for water, brown for sand and green for grass. They also experimented with using the cloths to create costumes for themselves, and then transformed them into a range of objects in different improvisations. A length of cloth became a rope used to pull someone out of a caved – in mine, with other cloths used to represent the walls of the mineshaft. Finally, we asked the participants to create whole environments using just their bodies in freeze-frames and movement. One member of a group became a person working in an office while the rest of the group created the shapes of desks and chairs, others used shape, sounds and movements to represent doors that opened and closed. Another group devised a prison scene where the group members formed the bars and the door of the cell, which opened to let a person in and then closed again.

The students were particularly enthusiastic in this workshop and became increasingly sophisticated and creative in their transformations. Freed from the struggle with a language not their own, and excited by the imaginative possibilities of transformation, they responded to the activities with real energy and concentration. This was particularly true in the final, extended improvisation where groups were asked to create and perform a dream or nightmare of their own choice using the cloths, chairs and their own bodies. The dream and nightmares that were portrayed ranged from childhood nightmares of monsters to adolescent fantasies of being super models. Significantly, in spite of including the possibility of portraying a nightmare, there were no improvisations dealing with the experience of being a refugee, although there were some violent nightmares very much in the genre of horror movies.

The students willingly performed for the rest of the class, and the improvisations made really effective use of mime, movement and transformation. In addition, almost all participants demonstrated a sustained commitment to their presentations. In reflecting on these presentations, the research team noted that one group of Burmese girls used dance movement from their culture to depict their dream of heaven, while an African group used a combination of storytelling and stylized movement which they later explained they had learnt as children.

At a planning meeting during this phase, we discussed the fact that when working in pairs or groups, the students had consistently chosen to work with other students of the same culture and gender. Despite this, there appeared to be a genuine level of engagement and enjoyment developing with each successive workshop, and both our observations and informal interviews indicated the students were becoming more confident and active. We decided to structure cross-cultural groups for a number of the activities, placing the English-speaking African students with the less fluent Asian students. We sought the approval of the students to do this, and in each session, group-forming games were played which we managed so that boys and girls from different cultures found themselves together in groups. After some initial resistance from both genders, this strategy was accepted by the students as part of the overall process, and led to more complex and structured group work investigating bullying. As a result of these strategies, the students chose to work in varied cultural groups more frequently, and there was a real sense of mentoring and assistance with language occurring. This was particularly evident in one group of girls where Maggie and Raylene (older, highly confident African girls) worked with Deela and Zema (younger Burmese girls who had been in refugee camps for almost 5 years and had little spoken English). The two younger girls were, not surprisingly, very shy and passive in the first two workshops, but this changed when the four girls chose to work together over a number of weeks. They became both really enthusiastic and highly focused in using drama to explore bullying. Maggie and Raylene dominated the initial group work, but also mentored and assisted the Burmese girls both with language and with using drama. As a result during the following weeks of the project, Deela in particular became more engaged and more assertive, and in an interview the girls suggested that they gained enjoyment and also learnt from the process:

Raylene: I learn that, . . . to stand up for yourself when someone is bullying you.

Maggie: I learn that bully is not good and if you hurt . . . if, if you bully somebody it hurt their feelings –

Maggie: And it's not nice.

Deela: Emotion

Interviewer: Yes.

Deela: Emerging, that thing. And then types of bullying. Specific . . . ah, is that . . . ?

Deela: Physical!

Interviewer: Physical. Yes.

Deela: Ya. The stuff, before I don't even know.

The power of peer teaching as a key component of the Acting Against Bullying structure is demonstrated here, for in this grouping of girls from different cultures and with different experiences, informal peer mentoring was clearly helpful in assisting Deela and Zema to achieve knowledge about bullying while also potentially developing their language and drama skills.

By the end of the first phase of the project then, our observation notes and the filming revealed that the students were freely and enthusiastically engaging in a range of drama exercises, activities and improvisations. After their initial reluctance to perform for the rest of the class, the students had increasingly become more verbal and more expressive in performance, and often vocal in demanding that they have the opportunity to show the other students their rehearsed improvisations. Jenny noted in an interview at this stage: 'Initially they found it very difficult to improvise, but now they actually have to be stopped because the improvisations run on and on.'

In fact, it seemed to us that at this stage there was very little observable difference between these teenagers from refugee backgrounds and any of the thousands of adolescents who had previously done the Acing Against Bullying programme in terms of enthusiasm, engagement, drama skills and understanding of conflict and bullying. Our planning for the second phase therefore focused on developing the expertise of the participants in conflict and bullying management through drama and enhanced Forum theatre. We also planned to prepare them for the peer teaching that was to come in phase 3.

Phase 2: Learning to Act Against Bullying

As well as the skills of conflict and bullying management, spoken language development continued to be a major focus of the second phase of the project, and we encouraged this through a process of immersion in improvisation and in the speaking of English, in and out of role. Because the original English language levels of the students ranged from strongly competent to almost no spoken English at all, we tried a number of different dramatic approaches to encourage language use. We discovered that the drama technique that most empowered the young people to speak and act confidently in public was the improvisation and performance of personal stories. Storytelling was the technique Liebmann (2004) used in her arts approaches to conflict with mainstream classes of teenagers, and it proved to be particularly effective for us in this second phase.

One experiment in storytelling had particularly powerful outcomes. Because language was proving to be a major barrier to performing narratives for many of the students, in one workshop we encouraged them to work in their language groups to improvise and perform a play in their own language, dealing with an experience of conflict or bullying. No guidance was given about whether the experience should come from the past or the present, and in fact, one group did choose to revisit an experience from childhood, while the other groups dealt with recent or current experiences. Working in their own language groups the students told each other stories of conflict and bullying. From these stories, scenarios were created of bullying situations the students were interested in exploring. These scenarios were turned into group performances in the language of the members of the group and later shared with the rest of the class.

A number of the groups performed their stories with enthusiasm and confidence, and in an interview afterwards they explained how being able to act in their first language gave them both a sense of confidence and a stronger sense of self. It also appeared to enable them to reconnect to some extent with the values of their own cultures in regard to unacceptable behaviour, but also to identify some attitudes that were at odds with aspects of their new lives and its associated cultural norms. For example, during this workshop there was some disagreement and disharmony in one group of African students where they initially claimed they all spoke Swahili but later determined that there were two different first languages spoken by the boys and girls in the group. The conflict appeared to be as much about gender as language, and this was part of the recurring theme of the struggle for inequality between the genders in the group. Nadia, our research officer, encouraged the group to reflect on the causes and nature of this conflict, and the girls in particular identified the dominant male ideology from their culture which they claimed caused the gender clashes between themselves and the boys.

Despite this incident, the majority of the other participants became increasingly confident and articulate about their ability to deal with conflict and bullying. By the end of the phase the students appeared to be confident with their knowledge of conflict management and bullying, and were able to apply that knowledge to the bullying situations that they were improvising. They also seemed to be capable of adopting all three roles in a bullying event including that of the bully, bullied and bystander. These perceptions were confirmed by the questionnaire, where the vast majority of the students stated that based on their experiences within the first two phases of the project, they were now more likely to do something to intervene in a bullying situation than they had been before the programme. Several also expressed a fear of bullies, noting that they were concerned that a bully may retaliate against a bystander for stepping in.

In the interviews at this stage even the students with the most limited English were eager to explain what they had learnt about bullying and how to manage it. When asked what they had learnt about bullying in an extended group interview, responses included:

Han: I learnt about bullying, it's, it's not good. And when you bully someone. . . . So, ya.

Peta: I learn about bully, there are many types of bully, like physical, social, and . . .

Han: Verbal –

Peta: Verbal, and cyber. If someone bully you sometimes you get too much angry, you sometimes, you try to bully back to them. . . . And yes, that's all.

Later in the same interview, when asked to identify what they had learnt about how to deal with bullying the following responses were typical:

> **Han**: . . . you can tell someone and you don't have to do something bad to yourself. And you have to tell your parents, teachers, friend.
>
> **Peta**: And like, if they, if they bully to you but you are alone, they bully to you but you never speak out to someone it always hurt you and then like, like are you a stupid person. Something like that. And then we don't speak out, just keep it –
>
> **Sans**: In our heart.

Importantly, these young people had also developed a vocabulary for describing bullying situations, including the various roles such as bystander. In addition, they were revealing through these interviews their growing understanding of power and motivation in bullying situations and its relationship to self-respect:

> **Peta**: If we saw a group of bully, like, we want to help but sometimes we're also scared. Like we sometimes, we could say 'Stop, don't do that'. Like, you know when we say the bully, they're not respect you and they don't listen to you, what you are saying. And what is the bystander feeling.
>
> **Han**: And they have. . . . They think they have much power. They kind of show off.
>
> **Peta**: Yes.
>
> **Han**: Yes, I think. Because they're. . . . Because they should, they can stop it. Some people bullies and they can't respect you, so you have to tell them and then they start respecting you and they will stop.

Even the students with limited English had developed a vocabulary and a set of appropriate actions that they might use when responding to bullying situations. For example, the interview below conducted with three recently arrived Burmese boys revealed some useful understanding:

> **Interviewer**: In what way has it (the programme) helped?
>
> **Tan**: We can tell our teacher or our parents . . . we can tell our friends, adults.

Azo: When someone want to bully you and then you like tell your friend, you have to control your friend, you have to say . . . you have to speak stuff to him. . . .

Gi: When you see the bully you can go and say stop, but you can tell your teacher and your friend. The police. . . .

The commitment to learning about conflict and bullying that had become apparent in this phase also seemed to fuel a sense of commitment and connection to the school itself. For example, Zema revealed this commitment by articulating her unhappiness at vandalism that was occurring at the school. This increasing sense of belonging to the community was noted by Jenny, the class teacher, and was an indicator of her developing sense of ownership of her new environment.

By the end of phase 2 then, the participants were demonstrating much greater confidence and apparent expertise in dealing with conflict and bullying, revealed through interviews and more importantly in action through the drama. They had become quite proficient in using improvisation and enhanced Forum theatre to investigate ways to de-escalate bullying, and their dramatic work increasingly explored a range of conflicts and all forms of bullying in many different contexts. We also observed what appeared to be a growing sense of self-esteem for some students and improved use of English to communicate ideas in an expressive manner. These outcomes were confirmed by the interviews with the students, the teacher and the support staff in the unit.

Phase 3: The struggle to peer-teach

At the beginning of the final phase of the research, in the last month of the project, we asked the students if they were willing to share their knowledge and expertise about bullying and conflict by peer teaching a Year Eight class in a series of workshops. The task involved not only the teaching of the concepts and the use of improvised drama, but also the preparation and staging of enhanced Forum theatre plays where a bullying situation is portrayed. During these improvisations, Year Eight students from a general class would be invited to intervene as one of the characters to de-escalate the bullying. Given the challenging nature of this task, there was not surprisingly some initial reluctance among the students, but they eventually agreed to do the peer teaching on condition that Jenny, Nadia and the young research assistants helped them to plan and practise. The entire team therefore took on the role of advisers and guides for the students as they prepared their peer teaching.

In spite of this support however, the first of the peer-teaching sessions was extremely difficult in terms of communication and cultural interaction, particularly because the Year Eight class included a number of students with behavioural problems. As such, even with the assistance of the facilitators, the peer-teaching students had problems making themselves understood and obtaining the cooperation of their peer learners with the result being that they completed the formal teaching they had planned within 20–30 minutes of the hour-long class. This problem had arisen previously in the early stages of other Acting Against Bullying programmes, however in this context, the problem was more acute. This was in spite of the fact that their teacher Jenny had devoted considerable class time to assisting the students in the planning of their peer teaching.

After this initial peer-teaching episode, a number of the participants expressed dismay and frustration that they had not been able to communicate effectively with the Year Eight students. The lack of attention and respect shown by the younger students had also made them feel inadequate. We therefore held a planning meeting with the whole group of students to determine if they wished to continue or not. All of them were adamant they wanted to complete the peer teaching but they realized they needed to restructure their approach. We reminded them that one group of the peer teachers had initiated a number of drama activities in the first session, both demonstrating them and setting up improvisations for their peer learners, and as a result the Year Eight students in that group had become re-engaged and enthusiastic. The other peer-teaching groups decided to adopt this strategy and did so with success.

In the following session, small groups of our participants, acting as peer teachers, performed their Forum theatre plays for their peer learners and invited them to intervene by replacing one of the characters in the action of the plays and deal with the bullying being portrayed. The plays themselves were effective in demonstrating different bullying scenarios, and in engaging the Year Eight audience. There were several significant interventions by the peer learners in each group and all involved genuine attempts to resolve the bullying. There was also some worthwhile discussion generated between the peer teachers and the peer learners about effective strategies for managing bullying.

The students were much more positive about the outcomes of this session of peer teaching, and there was a clear sense of accomplishment and self-confidence expressed in the planning session that followed. The secondary students discovered they were able to perform their forum plays effectively for the Year Eight class and to lead reflective discussions on the issues and consequences of bullying.

The final workshop saw the students assisting the peer learners to prepare their own peer teaching. Our observations and the film of this session show it was far less successful than we had hoped because the students did not have the pedagogical skills or the language to teach this component effectively. Much more time was needed to provide the students with effective teaching strategies and class-management techniques. The students themselves recognized this, and it was one of the recommendations made by them for any future iteration of the programme.

Nevertheless, a group composed of African and Burmese males was very positive about their peer teaching while acknowledging the difficulties they encountered. Ali was particularly positive about the experience:

Interviewer: So you all enjoyed teaching the class. What was your favourite part about teaching the class next door?

Ali: Well I enjoyed everywhere. I enjoyed being the host, and to direct, how to help my friends, to make the play up, to learn a thing, outside making the play, to explain to the students we teaching, what's happening and asking questions. I enjoyed doing that, I was so happy and shouldn't be a bully. When I was doing the bullying and then with this assistance how bullying started and how it gets escalated and then keeps going. Then we shouldn't and then just us when it's started – 1, 2, 3 just like that how bullies get to us.

Interviewer: So what did you like about teaching the other class Tan?

Tan: Everything. It make me to know how to teach others.

In response to a later question, about their experiences as a peer teacher Ali once again shows his enthusiasm for this approach when he notes:

> **Ali**: Well, like the most important thing in school and it was my favourite thing to do is when someone teach me someone I tell other people it is really good you shouldn't do . . .

In including this peer-teaching phase, we had hoped that it might give the students the chance to form mentoring and friendship relationships with other students in the school, and enhance their learning and their self-esteem, as it had done in the hundreds of schools where Acting Against Bullying had previously been implemented. However, the peer teaching proved especially difficult for the students, particularly those who had very little spoken English. The class that they were given to teach was also problematic. It was only in the final session of the peer teaching that we observed indicators of success and the peer teachers themselves felt that they had achieved something worthwhile.

Discussion

Our case study involved the structured use of drama with a group of new arrivals in a sequence of drama workshops over a period of one semester. In particular, a range of drama-improvised drama approaches were used to explore the nature of conflict and bullying, with some of the participants using stylized moment from their own cultures to tell stories. A form of African storytelling was also used extensively, where narrators spoke or sang a story while the other participants performed the narration. Some of the drama improvisations were enacted in the first languages of the participants, while others used a mixture of different languages in their work in a way that enabled them to feel confident.

The interviews we conducted with the students revealed increasing competence in dealing with fictional conflict and bullying scenarios but also, in some cases, with real bullying events in their lives. The students made it clear they believed that the peer teaching did benefit them despite the difficulties. They were more confident in their understanding of conflict and bullying and their ability to deal with it once they were placed in the role of having to teach the younger students.

The responses from students who completed the final questionnaire confirmed our observations and the comments made in interviews. Every one of the students involved indicated that they had enjoyed the project and identified significant learning from the experience, with almost every participant (92 per cent) being able to identify and explain at least one aspect or form of bullying. Students were confident that they could explain to a fellow student what bullying is and enjoyed demonstrating examples of bullying when peer teaching in order to provide a deeper learning experience. More significantly, 85 per cent of the students were able to identify the three stages of bullying in the order of which the stages occur and develop while 77 per cent of students were able to identify the three types of people in a bullying situation. Three of the six students who were not able to identify the three types of people in a bullying situation misunderstood the question and provided answers that actually addressed different questions regarding bullying such as the forms of bullying that occur. All the questionnaires were completed in class and Jenny and the student members of the research team were available to help, but they could only respond to requests for assistance in understanding the questions, and did not prompt the answers the students were giving.

Despite the limitations of their spoken English the students in the concluding interviews were able to identify key understandings about bullying and to confidently use the terminology. For example, one student noted:

> Bullying is when someone gets power over other people. Sometime more than one person bullying one person. They think they are the strongest people on the school.
> To physically, verbally, emotionally socially or cyberlly harm someone.

In describing what she had learnt about bullying from her involvement, Deela also revealed the significant other learning identified by the teacher:

> It's good we get to know how we can stop bullying, and drama is how we can stop bullying, and we act a bully, and everyone gets to know why we bully everyone. And what the bully feels. What the victim feels and what the bystander feels.

Here Deela clearly articulates her knowledge about the nature of bullying and conflict. This observation is remarkable for the confident and articulate way a student who was initially very passive and self-effacing and for whom English is her third language is able to express her ideas.

The majority of the participants shared Deela's confidence that they could now deal with bullying more effectively, and 77.7 per cent of them stated that they thought that bullying could be prevented, de-escalated or stopped. These students also demonstrated knowledge of the significance of the bystander in a bullying situation, and 81 per cent of them believed that the bystander was the most likely one to change a bullying situation. Students also put emphasis on telling significant people in power (such as parents, teachers and police officers) of bullying situations in order to prevent it from escalating. Responses included:

Because you can tell adult, teacher and parents that people are bullying you.

When the bullying can be prevented we can stopped it by saying that I will call police, and I'm went to complain to your mum and dad.

We can tell teacher, our parents or someone that we can believe they can stop bully.

Because the good bystander can stop them bullying the person and if they don't listen maybe the person who was a bystander can call the police and the police can stop the bullying.

Because a bystander can stop bullies and protect the victim from bullies and stand and stop bullied and some time they will be best friends or not.

An extended final interview conducted after the last workshop at the end of the project with a group of males that included students from Africa, Thailand and Burma provided useful indications of their learning and their growing sense of competence in dealing with conflict and bullying. Ali's enthusiastic and thoughtful responses offer the strongest example of the impact of this project:

Ali: Well, before I was don't know the different type of bully Like, but now I know many types of bully. How bully take place, and then how to solve bully. Like, before I don't know what is emotional, but I was not before, but not the way I know now. And then, I know what is physical. Ya, that's one I know.

Later in the interview he also notes:

Ali: Like, you know Sir I don't bully people. So because I've been bullied, I don't bully people here. But some people bully me. What's . . . when they bully me I have an idea how to solve it, to stop the bully so that they can't bully me any more. Ya.

I enjoy like, Acting Against Bullying. It's good and like it's to know about how to treat other people and know how to solve bully when it's happening, and I am happy the way they taught me, and they also taught me well. And I am so happy to know what is bully and how bully take this and how bully happen and how bully come to solve this and then how bullying gets worse. I learnt lots of things cos of bully and I am so appreciating for teaching me.

Tan was another young person who indicated within the final interview how the project had influenced his understanding of bullying:

> **Tan**: When I live in Thailand, the people come to kill me. They wanted to kill me and I start punch them. Now I don't do that anymore, when they want to make me angry then I just walk away.

Tan's reference to people coming to kill him was the first time any of the participants had ever indicated they had been in fear of their lives in the past. It is not clear how serious the threat was to Tan, but it does suggest the really serious nature of the conflict some of these young people had experienced before their settlement in Australia. What is significant for this project is the fact that Tan now feels he can cope with the threat of a conflict he is likely to experience in Australia much more effectively.

As well as the positive outcomes related to conflict and bullying, we had identified wider increase in knowledge, improved self-esteem and positive peer relations. Jenny identified four key outcomes from the project for the participants in terms of enhancing their settlement experience. She believed they were better able to identify conflict and bullying situations and know how to manage them; demonstrated an increased interest in, and commitment to, their schooling; showed an impressive development in their mastery of spoken English; and were able to realize that that they could change their behaviour not just in drama, but in the school and in their lives.

In our reflection on the outcomes of this particular work, the project team members working in this secondary school context concluded that the students had demonstrated very similar levels of learning about conflict and bullying as teenagers in the schools in Australia and overseas where Acting Against Bullying had been implemented in the past. We also believed that they had become just as competent as other students in managing conflict and bullying situations through drama, and in the case of Ali, in their own lives, despite their initial lack of experience. We were particularly impressed by their enthusiasm and engagement and how quickly they acquired a range of drama skills and then used them to investigate and change their responses to conflict and bullying. The struggle these students had with peer teaching was identified as far greater than in other projects, and we agreed that either far more time should have been devoted to preparing them for this aspect of the project or, given the lack of time, it should not have been attempted.

The very different life experiences and cultural backgrounds of these recently settled students certainly had a unique impact on the way they responded, but on the whole we feel that this enhanced the project. They brought to the discussions and the drama some fascinating viewpoints and complex experiences, and also a range of performance styles from their own cultures that enhanced the dramatic activity. We found their optimism, their desire to become part of the school and part of the society and their excitement for new learning enhanced the project and inspired the research team. Even the occasional clash of cultural attitudes between some of the boys and girls about gender equality generated interesting dramatic responses and lively discussion. The changes we observed in the students, changes they and their teacher confirmed in interviews, were definitely as positive and as significant as any we had encountered in all the other implementations of Acting Against Bullying. We believe that these changes were at least partly due to their backgrounds, and provide a strong argument for the use of applied theatre in forms such as Acting Against Bullying with teenagers from a refugee background.

One of the most valuable outcomes of action research is the way specific actions and strategies developed in one research context can lead to solutions to problems in other contexts. In this project the implementation of the Acting Against Bullying programme offered the opportunity to discover effective approaches to dealing with bullying

6

Passing the Sand: Integrating Arts and Language Pedagogies in a Further Education Context

It's Tuesday morning at 9am and class is due to start. Tuesdays are different to other days because visitors join the class for a couple of hours. Clusters of young people with long fringes, head scarves and corn row braids file into the demountable class room we have nicknamed the art annex, loops of white ear bud wires dangling around their necks. A short time later the group is arranged seated in chairs in a solemn circle. They are instructed that a small handful of sand is to be passed around the circle. As each bearer receives the sand it transforms – into honey, or a hot rock, or a kitten, or an ipod, or an apple – an object which is revealed by the way it is handled, and which then dissolves into sand again as it is carefully transferred to the next link in the circle. All eyes follow the sand with serene concentration as it makes its magical way around the circle. There is gentle laughter, murmurs of surprise and recognition. The focus is complete.

This chapter will explore a case study with new arrivals aged between 15 and 24, in informal and formal educational settings. The case study included a pilot project summer school created in collaboration with an arts organization and art gallery, and two further phases of action research in a TAFE language programme. What united the mini projects within the case study was an interest in exploring how to integrate multi-arts processes into fostering greater social confidence and enriching approaches to language learning. It was a developmental approach, grounded in the experiences and responses of the groups with whom we worked, and fuelled by a number of aesthetic hunches and instincts about how to approach language learning creatively. There were lots of mistakes, rethinks, over-planning, under-planning and happy accidents that led to a number of significant moments of connection and engagement. At the heart of the approach was a desire to explore and experiment with how to integrate different art forms into a process of meaning making that aligned with their English language curriculum. While at one level the goal of the project, particularly in the TAFE setting, was orientated to enhancing the curriculum, the arts project also sought to facilitate a process that supported negotiating the settlement process through storytelling and aesthetic representation.

As we progressed through the three phases of the project we began to learn more about the complexities and possibilities that emerge through the process of integrating art-based practices into formal programmes of refugee settlement support. The project revealed both the acute pressures on young people from a refugee background and their resilience, optimism and creativity in the face of these stresses. In this chapter we illustrate how drama can provide a performative context for a tentative pathway through the emotional turmoil of transition, growth and learning. Through the phases of the project we chart a dynamic, and at times unpredictable, interplay between aesthetic, emotional and learning experiences illuminating the way the young people move through the early stages of resettlement. In this process we identified three elements – aesthetics, emotions and learning – and describe how these functioned as feedback loops and entry points for moments of deeper engagement, creating the conditions for rich learning experiences.

Background

Unlike the case studies in the earlier chapters where the form was determined in advance, our practice and approach to how and what forms of arts practice we used shifted and changed throughout the process. As a facilitating team[1] we were very interested in exploring how multiple art forms like clay sculpture, art-making, digital technologies, dance and contemporary art could integrate with drama and theatre techniques to extend and deepen the learners' confidence in language. Our interest was to explore the texture of language through the interplay of art and drama processes.

In the first pilot study, we organized for a youth group (14–18) from MultiLink to travel to The Edge, a Brisbane-based venue that aims to provide the opportunity to explore creativity across arts, technology, science and enterprise. The youth group started with a tour of a new interactive exhibition at the nearby Gallery of Modern Art, and watched video work and installations, guided by the curator of the exhibition. The brief for the week was to create their own mini video exhibitions that would later be added to one of the audio-visual displays. The youth group then worked with a street dancer and choreographer, a rap singer and a film-maker to develop and edit their pieces for the Gallery exhibition. In the pilot study, we were keen to explore and open up to them the (free) resources and possibilities of different art forms including dance, music and film and validate their own work through public representation.

In the second phase, we worked with a TAFE group exploring some of the multi-arts ideas in The Edge project, but this time within the context of a language programme (Level 3). There were about 20 participants in this group, with very diverse language and cultural backgrounds. We worked with a highly experienced TAFE language teacher over seven weeks, once a week. We started with basic drama games and gradually built in language exercises as part of the improvisations and activities reinforcing vocabulary and grammar as we progressed. In this cycle we also used a collage activity using small cardboard boxes that were decorated to visually represent dreams and possibilities. The box art pieces were then used as the basis of both a live presentation and a short digital story.

In the third phase, we worked with another TAFE language programme (Level 2, low to intermediate English) over a 12-week period.

---

[1]   The main facilitating team was Michael Balfour, Nina Woodrow and Penny Glass.

In this project we developed a more considered structure of themes, drama games and role-plays and integrated this with music and clay sculpture work, an interplay which worked to extend and reinforce vocabularies, grammar and language confidence.

In this chapter we'd like to explore and illustrate how the practice operated, what was involved, but also how it links to the broader themes of the book. The chapter includes a montage of researcher notes, excerpts from interviews, lesson plans and participant feedback. Our intention in including material and data from such a range of sources is to share the way we accumulated a rich mosaic of information, stimulus, planning and reflection to arrive at fragile moments of inspiration and illumination.

The starting point of the TAFE mini projects was a keen interest in exploring hybrid aesthetic forms (drama, singing, photography, clay sculpture, dancing and visual art projects) and how these could align with implicit resettlement needs and explicit requirements for language learning. While government resettlement resources are focused on integration into work life (to become economically useful), there are also complex social needs at stake:

> Okay, work and the language is very important. But I personally don't think that even though one is very fluent in the language and has work they will be able to integrate. They are what you need to survive, but to become integrated you really need to feel it inside you and the majority also needs to absorb you, and I think that that is something that demands a lot of both groups. . . . (Westerling and Karvinen-Niinikoski 2010, p. 4)

The notion of a grounded participatory approach was key to the case study. In many ways our approach was tentative, exploratory, but there was always a governing principle of alertness to the way resettling participants were constructing their own personal, culturally meaningful, creative solutions to the particular circumstances that confronted them every day. In translating concepts of resilience into practice we encountered dynamics that were unfixed, evolving and fragile (Barber and Doty 2013; Lenette et al. 2012). Key to this was creating a safe and supportive atmosphere in the group that attempted to celebrate the uniqueness of an individual in a positive way, for example, by offering individuals the time and space to contribute to the workshop at their own pace. As with the other case studies the importance of partnerships with the TAFE teachers and reciprocity with the groups was critical in informing how the practice developed and our understanding of the dialogical environment.

Research approach

The reflexive and reflective approach to the practice informed the design of the research. The pilot study gave us a starting point about the needs and interests of the age group (14–18). For example, in the pilot study conducted at The Edge, the participants uploaded the short films they had made to social networking sites and were adept and hungry to learn more about technology. Many had networks covering Australia, their home countries, friends in refugee camps, and other friends who had been resettled in other countries. We did basic questionnaires and interviews with the pilot study group, as a way to understand how individuals responded to different aesthetic forms. The data and experience of running the pilot study gave us the interest in considering how to integrate multi-arts within a more formal language learning context, and inspired us to consider how an arts residency might work in a TAFE context.

The eventual shape of the project developed as a result of two phases of data collection, each involving weekly visits of 2 hours each across a term. Separated by a term, we worked first with a Level 3 youth group for 6 weeks, and then a Level 2 class for 12 weeks. We included short feedback sessions with participants, semi-structured interviews with the teaching staff, reflective journals of the facilitators, video and photography from the workshops, audio recordings of the facilitators' feedback sessions and artefacts from the workshops.

In this chapter we are interested in describing the work and drawing out some of the implications in relation to resettlement support, language pedagogy and multi-arts approaches. While the drama and multi-arts programme that resulted built on the learning that emerged from the pilot study, the orientation to research and programme design and development in this project was grounded in the work itself, drawing on an action research and phenomenological approach. The complexity and potency of using drama and arts with young people from refugee backgrounds is certainly fertile ground for analysis and further research, as the reflections and new learning that emerged from this project suggests.

The pilot study – Dance, rap and digital films

The aim of the pilot project was to experiment and integrate different forms of art processes into a positive and engaging intensive summer school for a group of MultiLink participants. The summer school attracted 15 children, from Burundi, Ethiopia, Eritrea, Karin Myanmar (Burma), Sudan and the Congo.

The pilot study was scheduled for the summer holidays and involved collaborating with a hip hop choreographer, a digital artist/film-maker and a rapper in partnership with The Edge and the Gallery of Modern Art (GOMA). At a basic level, the project was about promoting the availability of free accessible venues, and building the awareness of community resources that the group could continue to use after the project. Although Brisbane and Logan are close (40 km easy access by bus or train), it is unlikely that any of the participants were aware of or had ever been to Brisbane before. It was also important to ensure that the process was an invitation to engage and promote settlement by giving the group an opportunity to present their work online and at the Gallery. The enormous kick the group got from seeing their work completed and in the GOMA installation and shared with friends on social media was considerable.

The pilot study began with an invitation by the GOMA exhibition curator to make some work for a digital exhibition space. The exhibition was called '21st Century: Art in the First Decade' and featured selections from the Gallery's contemporary collection. The exhibition showcased works from Africa, the Middle East, Europe and North, South and Central America, Asia, The Pacific and Australia. It included a work in neon by Tracey Emin (England), sculptures and photographs by Romuald Hazoumè (Benin), playful sculptures of camp dogs by Arukun artists, including Arthur Pambegan Jr and Craig Koomeeta (Australia), powerful photographs by Mitra Tabrizian (Iran), Guy Tillim (South Africa) and Olaf Breuning (Switzerland), a suite of drawings by Frédéric Bruly Bouabré (Ivory Coast) and striking video works by SUPERFLE X (Denmark) and Sharif Waked (Palestine). The exhibition provided a fascinating and, in many cases interactive, playground of inspirational ideas.

The curator invited the participants to imagine their live and/or digital work in one of the spaces. The participant group then undertook a treasure hunt through the gallery to find ten specific pieces of work, and to record their responses. They then picked three of their favourite pieces and recorded their comments and reflections on them. After the visit we sat down and reflected on the visit to the Gallery. Far from being overawed by the scale and complexity of the exhibition, the group was full of ambitious ideas and ready for the challenge that had been set for them. Inevitably they had loved some pieces and found others 'boring'. Candice Breitz's *King,* featuring several Michael Jackson fans singing and dancing to tracks from *Thriller* (usually very badly) was a favourite. The collaborators and group members discussed how to develop the possibilities amidst a mountain of chaotic chatter and drawings on flip chart paper. We also talked about how to integrate the ideas with some of the new skills they would be exploring in the next few days.

The second morning was spent reviewing the ideas generated by their visit to the gallery, and then learning some basic hip hop moves and sequencing them into a routine. Once the routine had been learnt, each of the young people worked in pairs adding a further movement that could be integrated into the dance piece – therefore combining standard routines with the participants own dance movements. There were mixed dance skills in the group, but the facilitator was careful to go at a steady pace. The rapping facilitator was also careful to introduce basic rules of form and then allow the participants to build in their own creative content. The basic structure of rap is like simple poetry and in the group we explored the form and spontaneity of responding to call and response lines: 'What's your name? Where you from? What you doing? Pass it on.' After doing this in a round as a group, the participants then had some time to use this structure to write up lyrics and perform these back to the group.

As the mini rap songs and dance sequences developed, some of the group explored filming and learning how to edit each film on the computers in the lab, resulting in the production of eight short films that we then shared online via social networks and also presented in the GOMA space.

The pilot study was hopelessly ambitious and busy. The raw idea of creating opportunities for participants to engage in contemporary art viewing, engagement and participation in multiple arts was sound, but in its execution the process was a little incoherent and the quality

Figure 7 Filming the dance.

of the integration of different aims was often unfocused. While the participants had a rich mixture of experiences, and clearly had an enjoyable week, we felt that potential learning opportunities were lost in the rush. Nevertheless, the week provided us with an opportunity to see that multi-arts approaches could work if more carefully integrated and with clearer learning objectives. It was a question of harnessing some of the creative chaos into a more meaningful intercultural experience.

In reflecting on the pilot project, a number of lessons emerged for the facilitating team:

1. The use of technology as a transformative tool. All the participants were active and able in using social media and the internet. The participants all had social media accounts and uploaded and shared these with their friends and relatives in Australia, countries of origin, refugee camps and other resettlement countries. Recent research in Australia has underscored the value of participation in online social networks for young people from refugee backgrounds. Digital communication can support a creative capacity to engage in cultural renewal and reconstruction, to manage the delicate task of maintaining and reinventing local and transnational social identities (Wilding 2012).

2. The importance of being active producers of their work. The participants gained a number of skills and developed existing ones. They responded enthusiastically to the central tenet of creating opportunities to understand and manipulate different technologies and art forms.

3. The concept of resilience in practice. The pilot study demonstrated that the conceit of resilience building was rather naive. In many different ways the individual participants demonstrated that creative projects were not necessarily about *establishing* resilience, but about revealing and reinforcing it. Playfulness was an important imperative in the practice, a way of resourcing the resilience rather than constructing it.

The pilot project guided our reflections and planning for the next two phases. As the other case studies developed in the primary and secondary sector, it was intriguing for us to extend the experience of working with young people from a refugee background in a related but distinctive educational context. After a period of consultation it became clear that there was considerable interest and potential in developing a partnership in the TAFE sector.

The TAFE projects

We ran two phases of practice and research in a TAFE institution. Phase 1 was conducted with a Level 3 English Language youth group in April–June 2012 and the next phase with a Level 2 English Language youth group in February–June 2013. The student participants were aged between 18 and 24 years of age and all had only recently arrived in the country. In addition, all but a few had entered the country through Australia's Refugee and Humanitarian programme.

The intention with the TAFE phase of the case study was to design and investigate how a drama and multi-arts initiative could support resettlement through the introduction of creative forms of expression and communication. Although the research methodology and approach was geared towards remaining genuinely open to discovering new knowledge through reflections and observations of how these young people experienced the programme, there were a number of sensitized concepts that guided the work. In others words, as the project team members planned and facilitated sessions, gathered data and reflected on the implication of this data, we were sensitive to input that could help us answer questions about how drama and multi-arts could contribute to this programme in terms of enhancing well-being and resilience, language acquisition and social connections between peers.

Attendance in the two groups was never stable. Over the few months we worked with the group some students progressed to other levels and moved to a new class, while others were offered paid work in the fast food industry or on a factory production line. Some found it difficult to continue juggling family and caring responsibilities and were forced to, or chose to, suspend or cease their studies. Some of the students needed to take a break to address distressing health problems. In the phase 2 group and within the space of two terms (one half of an academic year), the membership of the classes changed significantly, with about a third moving on and with the total number of students fluctuating from about 20 to more than 30 for a couple of weeks in the middle.

The needs of young people and the Adult Migrant English Programme

In Australia, the Adult Migrant English Programme (AMEP) has a long history of providing initial English language instruction to immigrants and refugees. Refugees have a general entitlement of 510 hours for those who arrive through the humanitarian entrants programme with less than functional English. In 2004 this provision was extended for young people between the ages of 16 and 24 who can now access a further 400 hours of English language instruction.

The AMEP has adapted to the issues involved in supporting the various waves of new migrants to Australia, and to changes in leading theories of language acquisition and second language pedagogy. Over the last few decades the programming within the AMEP has evolved from a learner-centred curriculum negotiated between learners and teacher, to a competency-based national framework (Murray and Christison 2010). The focus in the AMEP is on settlement support rather than on developing proficiency in English language per se and the current national curriculum is aligned with a Quality Training Framework that regulates all training and educational qualifications in Australia (Kim et al. 2012).

The curriculum used in the AMEP is based on the Certificates in Spoken and Written English (CSWE) that employs an approach based on systemic-functional grammar and a social theory of language

(Murray and Christison 2011). The CSWE framework has a number of levels, including a preliminary stage that now accommodates lower literacy levels. Teachers then have the responsibility of translating this framework into classroom activities. As Murray and Christison (2011) explain, the curriculum is organized around texts (both written and spoken) that learners need to acquire, but the classroom teacher is responsible for devising and sequencing learning activities to put this curriculum into action since

> instructional content and methodology for helping learners achieve such acquisition are decided at the centre level or classroom. They are not provided in the curriculum framework. However, most AMEP teachers use the teaching learning cycle to present new language and have learners practice it. . . . Competencies are assessed as learning outcomes, with learners needing to produce the components of the text within the required time to be assessed as having achieved the outcome. (p. 129)

Customizing instructional content and the teaching/learning approach to the needs of different student groups is seen as a critical factor in the implementation of the CSWE curriculum. Recent research has sought to articulate the characteristics of the youth cohort as learners in AMEP classrooms and identify what distinguishes them from older students. For example, a 2008 study showed that these students

> tend to have a very strong orientation to peers of their age group and an awareness of various aspects of youth culture that are not of great interest to older learners. Younger learners are often less able to formulate goals for themselves and are often less aware of options open to them and pathways to access and achieve goals they may have. For young refugee learners with limited formal education, as well as limited English language and literacy skills, accessing mainstream vocational training and education is a challenge. (Murray and Lloyd 2008, p. 14)

Moore et al. (2008) underscore the presence of distinctive emotional needs among this cohort and 'a generally intense need to interact with their peers' (p. 34). This need is illustrated through interviews with teachers who report that 'they are not like adults, who will come in and are happy to spend a few hours learning English. It just doesn't work with those students. They need to be totally engaged. They need to be with other young people' (Moore et al. 2008, p. 66). Moore et al. also outline some of the pressures that affect this cohort in particular, and how this may impact on their learning within the AMEP. Stresses include: aftershock from past experiences, living and family situations, adjusting to Australian life, coping with adult responsibilities, and depression (p. 35). The study notes that teachers observe how students are often beset with 'worry and guilt about leaving loved ones behind who may be ill or almost certainly needing financial support' while they also experience complex stresses in their living circumstances. The conclusion here is that 'within the AMEP, the learning needs of refugee youth with minimal/no schooling are best met by youth-specific programs. . . . AMEP youth classes are both feasible and highly desirable, although demanding of teachers and administrators' (Moore et al. 2008, p. 35).

The existing research therefore, has highlighted some tensions between the national curriculum framework and the particular needs of young people from refugee backgrounds. Although the AMEP is founded on a social theory of language, it is implemented within a credentialled, competency-based Vocation Education and Training (VET) system, and a casework model for settlement support, which is highly individualized. Efforts to articulate the needs of this cohort have consistently highlighted the benefits of offering these students pathways into various social roles, employment, further educational opportunities, cultural and sporting pursuits, opportunities to develop emotional connections with peers and durable, supportive, social networks. An approach to language learning and settlement support that acknowledges individuals past experiences, cultural and linguistic background along with their developmental stage is recommended. In other words young people from refugee backgrounds are more likely to flourish in dedicated youth programmes that draw on holistic,

UNIVERSITY OF WINCHESTER
LIBRARY

community development and transformative models of adult education (Onsando and Billett 2009).

In our TAFE project the classroom teacher spoke about how she had adapted the programme to recognize the specific needs of young newly arrived students:

> [w]e have a big youth programme here. One of the biggest in Australia and something we try to do regularly is to take them all out somewhere. We have a big day out . . . we have picnics . . . and we do ridiculous things . . . we play musical chairs . . . we do egg throwing . . . three legged races because they have never had a childhood . . . a lot of these people . . . and one young girl said to me oh miss can we do running races . . . and I said why. . . . I was never allowed to run when I was a little girl in wherever . . . and you think they have never been kids . . . they have been supporting their families in camps and things . . . foraging for whatever they can get . . . competing for whatever they can get since the time they were born . . . so we let them be kids sometimes.

At the same time, however, the excerpt below shows how teachers in this programme are also responding to the onerous burden these young people carry to succeed:

> if we are having trouble with a group we will ask for some special help . . . (we) brought in some people (from a counselling programme for survivors of torture and trauma) to talk about our Afghani boys . . . the Maritime arrivals . . . and the issues that they would be dealing with . . . the fact that someone had spent a lot of money to get them here . . . the expectation that they would bring the whole village after them and of course that's just not going to happen . . . so how do we deal with that anger . . . that desperate need to get a job that we are seeing in the classes . . . and so we do reach out for (professional development) as a local individual group if we need to.

Our experience of partnering with TAFE teaching professionals was their impressive commitment to covering the curriculum while also responding to the implicit needs of the young people. It was clear that the teachers were under enormous pressure to deliver and measure the implementation of a structured curriculum. The national reform agenda that swept through the VET sector in Australia in the 1990s had profound impacts on the culture of the workplace and the practice of English language teaching in this setting. The agenda has shaped the way the work of TAFE teachers is managed and perceived by teachers themselves. It has created a VET workforce that is characterized by the skills-based industry trainer as the normative model informing investment in the development of teaching expertise and culture in VET (Seddon 2008).

The tension here, as some commentators have pointed out, is that TAFE teachers have historically aspired to a service ideal and a professional ethic that gives primacy to the learner. As Chappell (1999, p. 8) explains: '(t)eachers in TAFE have taken on the discourses of liberal education in the construction of their identity. They construct themselves as educators who are interested as much in the humanistic goals of individual and social development as they are in industrial skill development.' This is arguably even truer for teachers working with migrants and refugees than anywhere else in TAFE. A teacher in our project, for example, talked about her belief that the young people need to be recognized as individuals, i.e. these students require more than language instruction to achieve success. When asked what she saw as critical in helping students to survive this period of transition and despondency, she replied:

> I think it is support. And encouragement to show them that they do have a future, and there is a hope . . . and show them pathways of how to get to where they want to go . . . just encourage them . . . and I think we honour each and every student, and we value them as people, and we . . . it's something we do . . . because we believe . . . we believe in them . . . and we try to show that in everything that we do, that they are important, and although it's hard for them now, you know, keep in there, keep at it, and they will get better . . . most language teachers have an empathy for these students, and I think that's why

they're here, because they do go that . . . above and beyond just teaching them language . . . and I think it's important for them (to be treated as individuals with something to contribute, individuals who need support to be who they are and who they can be) especially the backgrounds they've come from . . .

out of the refugee camps where they've been a nobody, and being that minority and persecuted . . . especially the girls, and instill in them, you know, some self-esteem.

In sum, within an environment marked by a rapid shift to an industry led and entrepreneurial workplace culture, many TAFE ESL teachers have nonetheless retained, as part of their professional identities, a vital interest in the well-being of their students in a holistic sense, and therefore hold on to a personal degree of responsibility for creating meaningful and empowering learning experiences for their students. Ollerhead (2012, p. 616), in her study of the practice of teachers working in TAFE with students from refugee backgrounds with low levels of literacy, has documented cases of 'successful micro level contestations of policy, in the form of transformed teaching' that 'allows for a re-conceptualization of a view of teachers as a passive recipient of policy (and) enables a focus on the highly variable capacity of teachers to utilize their agency to both resist constraints and capitalize on enablement's in their individual classrooms and teaching environments'.

In the context of TAFE policy and practice, we found that the teachers who we worked alongside were operating out of a sense of their vocational identity as professional educators, rather than contracted trainers, and it was this impulse that motivated their effort to embrace a partnership in this instance with arts practitioners, resulting in the two phases of the TAFE project. For both partners, however, the tensions inherent in the policies and practices framing the delivery of language instruction and settlement support in this context, constrained what was possible and consequently, compromised what we were able to offer the participants. One example of this is the ways that timetables are managed that prioritize administrative efficiency over the needs of the students and teachers. The comments below suggest that the teacher struggled at times with assessment requirements and timetabling limitations that conflicted with her impulse to articulate her own classroom planning and teaching practice with the flow of the drama and art-based work:

> It was difficult mainly because of my class and me because I'm a full-time teacher but I have the other role that I do. . . . I'm only in class 2 days and then I have a tutor one day and then another teacher the last day and so I have taken responsibility for a module and it was a big writing module last term . . . we were writing our opinions . . . and I felt that on Tuesday we did lots of the speaking, the oracy and so on . . . we did lots of vocabulary development with you but on Wednesday I really had to get down and get the writing done . . . and so I felt I didn't do justice to the programme . . . whereas if I had them over the four days myself I would have followed up with some of the things we've done in class . . . I could've had more time . . . I wouldn't ask the tutor or someone to do that because they didn't know what we have done . . . so I feel that was a drawback . . . but it was my fault . . . it was probably not the best class to do it with in the sense of a four day teacher on the same . . . with the same teacher would've done . . . would have got more value for the students out of what we did . . . I think . . . if we did it again we would have to make sure it was much better incorporated into the learning as a whole so that they could see the value of it but as I said it was just really the limits of my timetable which meant that I didn't do it as well as I could've done.

The participants

The participants in our TAFE project were culturally and linguistically a very diverse group and their social circumstances also varied considerably. While some young people had arrived with their families, there were a number who had arrived independently as separated children, or unaccompanied minors. The participants had either been sent alone to

Australia for their own protection or had lost their families as a result of war. Government reports indicate that the number of children (under 18 years of age) arriving in Australia as irregular maritime arrivals (i.e. they came by boat without a visa) has increased steadily over recent years and that most of these arrivals are teenage boys from Afghanistan (Multicultural Youth Advocacy Network 2012).

Many of the most recent arrivals in Australia in this age bracket have lived most or all of their lives in refugee camps or in other places of first asylum. The most recent arrivals include many who have come from parts of the world beset by protracted political conflict, such as Middle Eastern, Asian and African regions. Human rights, forced migration and trauma studies' scholars have noted the changing nature of contemporary warfare whereby civilian populations are increasingly vulnerable. This leads to a pattern of persistent detrimental effects on children and young people, since

> the changing tactics and technology of warfare have magnified hazards to children. Wars are increasingly fought within states and involve non-state actors, such as rebel or terrorist groups less likely to be aware of, or abide by, humanitarian laws providing for the protection of civilians. . . . As a result, modern 'wars of destabilization' often rupture the fabric of life that supports healthy child development. (Stichick and Bruderlein 2001, cited by Betancourt 2012, p. 1)

The young people in our study were survivors of both the direct and indirect effects of armed conflict. Indirect effects include upheaval and chaos in an entire region, along with 'the loss of a sense of security and predictability, the lack of structure in daily life, the shattering of family and community support networks, and the loss of the infrastructure that supports positive child development (e.g. when schools or water, sanitation or medical services are damaged or destroyed and disrupted)' (Robinson 2013, p. 195).

The young people we worked with had, for the most part, experienced personal histories with significant disruptions to wider social and cultural infrastructures vital for learning and development. Such life histories mean that many in our group had very limited or interrupted experiences of formal education. The effects of such impoverishment of their social ecology are especially acute for those who have arrived in Australia as unaccompanied minors. These young people are often facing the massive task of resettling in a new country quite alone, with some struggling to sustain material and emotional connections with family and community members remaining in their countries of origin. The impact of these stresses and strains were evident in our participant group. During our weekly visits students quite often complained of physical distress – back pain, headaches, viral infections and other illnesses – along with expressing concerns about absent family members, financial worries and anxiety about the future. The teacher of the class described some of the issues she had observed:

> [w]e had some very traumatized young Afghani boys for example recently . . . who have come by ship . . . and we noticed in our art work where they were drawing sharks and things . . . that this was a pretty traumatic journey for some of the boys . . . and when they come here they don't settle well . . . they can't sleep . . . and one of the girls in the class is having big problems and she's backwards and forwards to the doctor . . . she can't sleep . . . and every time she shuts her eyes something . . . I don't know what her background is . . . I've never asked her directly. . . . So she can't sleep . . . and this is years . . . she has been here several years so . . . and of course some of them are alone . . . a lot of them are unaccompanied minors . . . and say they are living in group houses where the dynamic is difficult . . . they are living with carers who perhaps don't always do things the way . . . as Australians . . . because often the carer is from the same ethnic groups so it can be difficult.

Further comments from this teacher also attest to a strong tendency for these young people (provided they are free from ongoing violence) to negotiate this challenging transition in a positive way:

> I actually got mine to map their culture shock once . . . and here is okay when you first heard that you had a visa to come to Australia . . . you first got on the boat how did you feel? . . . and of course we start at

very high and then after a few months we've got this homesickness and it's not all I thought and they won't get a job and there is no Mercedes which someone promised me and so we came right down low . . . then I will say at another time . . . and then so where are you now? . . . and it was interesting the difference points that they saw themselves as being . . . most saw themselves as being above the neutral line but interestingly some who have come as wives . . . spouses on spousal visas . . . were, I think, experiencing some domestic violence issues or domestic conflict issues and were seeing themselves going downhill . . . whereas everyone else was tracking up.

Phase 1 – Adventures in multi-arts

The facilitator team for the two phases of the TAFE project was Nina Woodrow, an experienced TAFE language teacher and arts practitioner (and our research assistant on the overall research project), Penny Glass, an experienced community arts worker, and Michael Balfour, an applied theatre researcher.[2]

Our starting point was Nina's interest and experience in teaching English as a second language, and her frustration with the increasingly restrictive frameworks of the competency approach in TAFE settings. As a team we were interested in exploring and experimenting with integrating drama with voice work, art-making processes, digital communication and language learning. Principally we were interested in exploring a process that involved cognitive, social and affective learning. With regard to the cognitive we wanted to help participants acquire new language in a meaningful context; with the social function, we wanted to use drama and the arts to increase the cooperative interaction among group members; with the affective function we wanted to explore how linking different aesthetic modalities (drama, role-plays, games, art

---

[2]   In the second phase, we also collaborated with Sarah Woodland, an applied theatre researcher, and Brea Robertson, an undergraduate on the BA Contemporary and Applied Theatre program, Griffith University.

processes) might produce a deeper and more engaged relationship to language. The multi-media approach was a way to explore the texture and meaning-making elements of language, to encourage students to enjoy and have fun with language. Our affective goal was to ensure a playful engagement with language and social confidence.

In the first phase we had a limited 6 weeks to go from building trust and confidence to developing digital reflective presentations (oral presentations were a required part of their curriculum). We worked closely with the TAFE teacher who ensured that issues covered in the workshop were followed up during other lessons in the week. We started with some basic drama exercises, such as name games (Name and an Action), energy games (Zip Zap Bop) simple improvisation games (What are you doing?), trust games (leading people around space with eyes closed) and some gentle voice work. We often used games that involved mime and silent images as a way to generate words and ideas. Often these games would produce new vocabulary for individuals – how did this exercise make you feel? – and we would stop and write words, expressions up on paper hanging around the classroom. Students would later record these words in their journals. Other times we would stop games to explain a term or expression, again giving time for students to make notes.

One of our first structured exercises was to ask the question 'what surprised you when you came to Australia?' exploring things they saw, and then asking the students to show the surprise physically but non-verbally. The other participants then had to guess what the actions were showing. This exercise generated both shared experiences of first arrival and felt expressive vocabulary that we systematically recorded on the paper hanging round the classroom. The participants then talked about the images and experiences and related those to their own. The TAFE teacher followed this up later in the week with a short writing exercise that captured some of these moments. We set up a Flickr account that included photos of the word and images of the workshop, and students were able to access this site and write responses to the images and use this as a resource.

We revisited the question 'What surprised you when you came to Australia?' and explored this in relation to sounds and smells, developing related creative exercises. For example, we divided the group into threes and they talked of sounds that surprised them and then shared the sound. We went on to create a piece of music with the groups and their sounds as sections of an orchestra exploring volume and pace.

In the third week the TAFE teacher asked us if we could explore symbols and metaphors. The teacher had said that the participants found it difficult to grasp concepts that were not literal. We went about designing a workshop that could explore some of these themes and also align with our idea for them to create a poem and perform it. Here is an account from Nina of the session that provides a vivid description of the workshop:

Nina's Research Journal

August 2012

Today we did the fourth of our sessions at Logan with the refugee youth class. Something clicked today and I am feeling good about how all this is working. We are improvising a workshop design that could eventually lead to producing a digital story – a set of activities that hopefully provide this group with the linguistic and symbolic resources to work out what they want to say and how they want to say it.

The art box idea worked really well. I had two reasons for wanting to try this approach, both to do with supporting a group of people from refugee backgrounds to tell stories in this new place, in safety, in their own term. One was about how useful objects are for inspiring storytelling, but this method is difficult with refugees since they almost always come with nothing, having lost this connection with their past. I wanted to see how it worked to create a memory box, an artifact that could work in a similar way. I also wanted to explore this device as a way to develop a symbolic language to represent experiences in a way that avoids an insistence on testimony.

I was worried at the last minute that some of the boys would not engage but they did. Amazing really. We introduced these little plain cardboard boxes . . . and a pile of magazines and other collage material. We pushed all the tables together and we spent most of the session sitting around the table . . . talking and decorating our boxes. We started the session with a drama activity, led by Penny that just set up the task of decorating the box so well. We stood in a circle, one little box on the floor in the middle. At first the task was to take turns to go into the middle and walk around the box till you 'saw' something in it, then take it out and 'show' it to the rest of the group, without words, till we guessed what it was . . . a snake, a ring, a book.

Then the instruction was that what was in the box now was 'your hidden talent'. This was a subject that had arisen from our earlier drama work exploring themes important to these participants followed by mapping and categorizing activities. So they showed us what they loved doing . . . singing, dancing, cooking, painting. . . . Starting with something playful that involves the whole group, works in ways I can't quite describe yet. Like an imaginary game, it produces a sense of child-like collusion in suspending disbelief and involving yourself in the idea that the box is magic . . . the box can hold something . . . the box can represent me. The power of theatrical approaches with this group of refugee participants was interesting to observe.

So with this premise established by the group . . . the magic flows on to the art . . . and the young people embraced the notion instantly. It was brilliant.

I do wonder about the symbolic power of a box and how truly cross cultural this form is – a vessel, an enclosed space, a holder – they are universally understood forms in both practical as well as symbolic ways. It doesn't seem to take much language to communicate the task, to link the idea of the box to the self and the inside space as a holder for something internal and the sides perhaps being aspects of that world . . . and the outside being the way you present yourself or the way the outside world impacts on you. The metaphor of the box for the self in this way was accepted easily.

The idea of the internal space representing an internal quality, a feeling, a story, a characteristic, an aspect of personality, dreams, aspirations, ambitions, goals . . . was embraced and adopted by the group . . . their boxes showed examples of these representations. These metaphors and symbols were frequently loaded with an emotional power. When we each presented our box and talked about its meaning, in a story circle kind of activity, you could see this emotional power in the body language and in the voice . . . and then the background information supplied by the teacher afterwards confirmed these impressions.

The workshop went from noisy chatter and drama games (social group chatter and competitive calling), through to setting out the art tables (scraping chairs and furniture), explanation, questioning that tailed off into concentrated silence during the art-making process (absorbed focus with occasional requests for tools and/or materials), and then the

Figure 8 Box 1.

Figure 9 Box insert.

Figure 10 The box and the story of the box.

quiet positioning of the box exhibitions around the space, until the final stage of each person talking about their box and the deeply attentive sound of everyone listening. There was a clear articulation between the drama and the box-making activity. The embodied pleasure of playing physically carried the energy through to the more reflective box-making activity and then onto the presentation of their work. One of the participants had pasted a volcano onto his box and when he was asked to describe why he had added the image, he searched hard for the right word. The rest of the group tried to help him out. He kept saying 'it's like . . . like . . .'. It was clearly a frustration for him not to communicate the metaphor. Then someone said: 'Like . . . molten?' And the participant jumped out of his seat in finally being able to name the feeling.

Kramsch (2008) addresses the role of facilitators as 'teachers of meaning' who need to

> build on students' memories, emotions, perceptions, fantasies linked to sounds, and intonations. Ask the student: What does the word evoke for YOU? What does it remind YOU of? Bring back the emotional and aesthetic dimension of language. (2008, p. 405, original emphasis)

The participants were then given the task of constructing a reflective poem that captured an interpretation of their boxes. The TAFE teacher did some further work with the participants in other lessons and the following week we rehearsed a short class presentation. The poem and pictures of the box were then uploaded to a digital story platform and included as part of the students' portfolios.

The TAFE teacher remarked on how important this phase of the project was, as the students were very driven and under pressure to learn English as quickly as possible, to get a certificate, to get a job, to send money back to their families/relatives. The pressure often proved counter-productive to language acquisition, making the students tense and impatient. The TAFE teacher observed that the arts process helped to

> bring out things in their personalities, like those hidden talents, and of course, we can . . . , they can be valued because of those things, and they could just be themselves, they didn't have to . . . they didn't have to be excellent students, or bent on getting their certificates, or finding a job for that period of time, and so they relaxed! And I think a lot of language was learnt through that process.

Our learning from phase 1 of the TAFE project was the following:

1. The imperative of play and social engagement. One of the qualities of drama/arts work is that it can increase and open up opportunities for different kinds of social interaction. As identified by the TAFE teacher and supported by the literature, young people from a refugee background can be under enormous pressure to resettle successfully and help and support other relatives and family members elsewhere. Creating the space to share stories and themes in an enjoyable and fun way helped to dissipate the feelings of pressure for a limited time. Indirectly some of students were able to become more confident in rehearsing language usage. The language was wrapped up in the playful activities, and also surfaced in the opportunity for participants to reflect on and share personal anecdotes. The workshops built on emotional and aesthetic dimensions of language.

2. The shortcomings of technology. For these young people, technology was used in a focused way, as an adjunct to support their presentation skills and requirements of the curriculum. In actual fact, we found that the technology absorbed a great deal of time and became much more individual rather than group focused and lessened the creative flow and energy. The digital stories were interesting, but a little bit of an anti-climax after the live presentations.

3. The importance of responsiveness and reflexivity. There were benefits in carefully integrating drama, language learning and art-making in partnership with the TAFE professionals. The more-focused partnership enabled the facilitator team to align the workshops to unit goals, but also to explore more affective areas of language learning and social relationships. It allowed for the exploration of imaginary scenarios as well as fixed-point conversational situations linked to a standardized curriculum. In other words the facilitators became more responsive and clearer about the purpose of each workshop, but remained responsive and reflexive to the issues that emerged as a result of the practice.

It was also clear that once a week for 6 weeks limited the potential areas of development and learning. We took these reflections into the next phase, designing a 12-week programme, but this time working with a Level 2 group.

Phase 2 – The art annexe

The second phase aimed to refine some of the ideas from our earlier projects. This was developed through focusing on three areas: group building, trust and individual confidence; speaking and writing, and vocabulary extension; and creative expression, play and improvisation (both with language and with roles).

In the first area, drama was the primary activity. For the second and third areas we employed a variety of language learning scaffolds (word wall, sand models) and art forms (music, visual art and poetry). Since membership of the group was quite unstable we found that we needed

Figure 11 Drama group work.

to return to the first area again and again to create the conditions necessary for risk-taking and creative extension.

In the first week we started with some basic warm up games, image theatre work and simple narrative-building exercises. The more basic language skills of this group required us to keep explanations simple, and ensure that we modelled games before we started them. It was also clear that there was confusion in the group about why we were coming in to the classroom and disrupting the normal routine. The energy in the workshop fluctuated greatly, and retaining focus and interest was challenging. We learnt to develop workshop plans that incorporated a mixture of high-energy games (competitive) that the students enjoyed, tempered with image based exercises and improvisations.

In the early workshops there was a degree of shyness, particularly among the girls. When we broke the big group into smaller groups there was a lot of support needed and a fair amount of scaffolding to get underway with an activity. Simple activities like the name game were appreciated, as the group had never learnt each other's names, and this seemed to break down the general feeling of shyness. One element of the success was the repeated use of one poetic phrase combined with small additional words. The TAFE teacher observed:

> I was really happy how the shy people, and there are quite a few very shy people in that class, were happy to stand up and speak. It's that worry that holds so many of them back. I think the drama programme released some of them from that because it was nonsense, it was games it didn't matter, it wasn't a teacher asking them a direct question. So I think it freed them. That's what I loved about it – the fact that they were talking gibberish, or they were explaining their painting or whatever they were doing. And the other thing I liked very much was the fact that everybody was expected to participate (interview with teacher).

We introduced the 'What surprised you about Australia?' activity exploring sounds and images. This elicited some funny observations. One participant had seen a dog lick his owner's face, something that he couldn't believe. A number of students found the absence of constant noise disquieting. The group members were used to hearing constant voices and human activity all the time. The quiet was unsettling. Another participant remembered seeing the Australian sea and being in awe of the sound and the power of the beating waves.

These stories generated a word wall of sensory vocabulary that we used and referred back to each week, encouraging students to explore the texture of these words and use them in their writing. We introduced a game of opposite words (dark–light, trust–belief, hard–soft) that explored differences and connections. We also developed a more structured and explicit approach to the workshops, generating a theme/aim that we introduced at the beginning of the session to clarify our purpose and link it to the other classes that the participants were doing.

Nina's Research Journal

May 2013

Half way through the program and, as facilitators, we are beginning to move and plan with a little more confidence and intuition. As a team with backgrounds in community development, language teaching, settlement support and arts and theatre, in various combinations, our quest in part, has been to find a form that successfully integrates disparate practices in a way that is customized to the needs of this group, and in a way that acknowledges what we are learning about their experiences and perceptions. My sense at this stage is that one of the most valuable things we are learning is how to improvise with pedagogical and aesthetic approaches, how to synthesize strategies in a way that allows the participants to engage playfully. Achieving this kind of engagement, with this group of over-burdened young people, is more challenging and crucial than it sounds.

Playful engagement, when we manage to make it happen, lowers the 'affective barrier' to language learning, it reduces anxiety, it creates a communally held container for safe individual expression. We have by now encountered enough dead ends, negotiated enough twists and turns in the road we were travelling together with this group of very diverse young people to develop some trust in our process. We are beginning to accept that although what we do won't always work, there is a series of steps we can take, a meandering path we can initiate that sometimes leads us there. We have developed enough of a sense of who they are, what they struggle with, to be able to begin consciously building imaginative new spaces for our work together. We are beginning to offer gestures, games, tools, playful moments that sometimes strike a chord. We build an aesthetic milieu that occasionally makes sense to them, and the invitation to stay present and engaged, to take a risk, to experiment, to play, is occasionally accepted, with surprising consequences.

The sessions each week included a theme to focus the work and link it pedagogically, albeit loosely, to the curriculum. In one of the sessions we introduced clay-making activities as part of the process, and linked them to the developing vocabulary the group were gaining. The clay exercise was inspired by a workshop initially developed by Monika Pagneaux, a French movement specialist in physical theatre. Like the boxes exercise in the previous phase, we were interested in how non-language-based activities actually generated and worked with drama work to both create and play with the exploration of language.

In the first part of the workshop we reviewed the vocabulary around emotions that had been generated previously (there was a list hanging on the wall). These were words like anger, fear/love, compassion, hope, despair, joy, hatred, worry, pride, shame, jealousy, etc. We played a role-play game with the words, asking teams to represent the words through gesture, expressions and postures (no words) and have the others guess what they were trying to show. This led to a game exploring postures in which the group learnt five words – lying, sitting, kneeling, half-rising and standing. Participants were asked to move around the space until one of the five words is randomly called and they adopt this pose and freeze.

Once the group had a small break we brought them into a circle to sit down. There was a small piece of clay and an A4 piece of paper on the floor in front of each participant. Participants closed their eyes and were told that they had 7 minutes to shape themselves in clay. Once the time was up they showed each other the sculptures briefly. The participants then looked at the vocabulary of emotions (from the list on the wall) and were asked to close their eyes once more and add one of the emotions to the sculptures in 9 minutes. After this task the participants were divided into groups of five. One person placed their clay sculpture on the A4 paper. In small groups the participants talked about what each figure might be feeling. Moving slowly, a second person added their sculpture in relation to the first. One at a time the other three people added theirs, taking time to consider each sculpture and their relationships and to talk about what story might be unfolding. The group then speculated on what was happening in the scene. Who are the people? Where are they? What is happening? What happened before? What will happen next?

From these discussions, the small groups were asked to improvise and rehearse a scene, and these were finally performed for the larger group. It was interesting to observe that this exercise offered a change in

Figure 12 Clay work.

focus and energy. For the first time, we noted a strong sense of presence among the participants. Like any workshop there are always ebbs and flows of attention and focus, but for this one, the contrast between high-energy activities that led to exercises that demanded quite intense individual concentration and then back into socially integrated activities really seemed to carry the group. The workshop rhythm really aligned strongly with the group's abilities and interests, and the result was a coherent and surprisingly emotional workshop.

The following week we followed this up with the theme painting a picture with words. After some high-energy games, we introduced some basic improvisation games. To further build on the vocabulary they needed to explore as part of the curriculum, we introduced a game exploring opposites. In this exercise a series of opposites are called out and each word is allocated to opposite sides of the room. Participants move to the right or left hand side of the room depending on which word they have an affinity for:

black/white
hot/cold
sweet/sour
past/future
quiet/loud
smooth/rough
day/night
fast/slow
awake/asleep
light/heavy
big/small

Participants were then asked to record the list of words they related to in their notebooks. We then introduced the idea of tangible/intangible word categories and generated a list with the participants, for example: Intangible: faith, forgiveness, determination, freedom, imagination, vulnerability, honesty, courage. Tangible: Animals, Landscape – mountain/river/desert. This led to a structured discussion about metaphors, and the participants were asked questions about: What colour would forgiveness be? What animal would freedom be? Is courage a mountain or a river or a desert?

After a short break we looked at some short YouTube poems created by African Somali (AS) refugees in NZ (video) (http://youtu. be/yHBdqhYmHrs). We discussed the poetry and how the poets had used a very simple rap structure, starting with the stem words 'I am ...'. We let the group know that we would be developing similar poems by the end of the session. The workshop then returned to the claywork, and as with the previous week, the participants had short amounts of time where they had to create a sculpture in response to some music. The participants each then placed their sculpture in the centre of an A4 piece of paper and stood up and walked round the other sculptures. Once they were ready they were asked to write 1–2 words on each paper beside the sculpture (these words could be drawn from

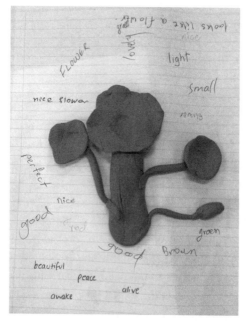

Figure 13 Clay plus writing.

emotional vocabulary, the opposites exercise, or other vocabulary) representing a feeling that the clay created. The participants then returned to their spot and reviewed the collection of words that their classmates had written on the paper. This collection of words along with other collected words in their notebooks were then used to write an 'I am . . .' poem. The poems were then performed to each other one by one.

Penny's Research Journal

> The clay sculpting sequence worked because it was built up throughout the whole workshop, there was a journey to it, and that gave time for people to understand its purpose, and there were multiple entry points ('busy hands', imagination, plasticity, vocab, poetry, etc). Themes came out without forcing and seemingly without self-censorship (war, soldiers with guns, fear and death) and an inclusive story was built by both groups. With this work, we experienced 'the thawing effect', the group felt like a group and the individuals entered the group space with ease, the sadness departed for a moment. There were peaceful faces during the clay work (the background music helped with this). All engaged more easily. There was pleasure in the concentration moments. There was joy in the sharing.

> With the poetry, introducing the activity with the 'AS video' (A.S. stands for African Somali. In the video we showed, a group of Somali refugees in New Zealand performed their own rap poems that were the outcome of a facilitated workshop using the 'A.S.' vocalization as a powerful rhythmical refrain. We modeled our work on this poetic device, using the refrain 'Y2G' which is the class descriptor Y = Youth, 2 = level 2 English and G = Class group). This video gave them a very clear understanding of what was expected, and led to creating our own structure for the rap. We also had done vocabulary building work previous to creating the rap: opposites, tangible/intangible, abstract nouns, colours, animals, metaphors, which provided the linguistic tools. For the performance we had one student encouraging the rest

to perform, and the whole group celebrating each performance. This was the first time the group functioned as a cohesive, self-managing community in this way.

Teacher Interview

They made their little clay models and they did it individually . . . they had their eyes shut, they couldn't see what other people were doing . . . and they weren't told to make part of the story or anything . . . it was just a purely individual thing . . . but then when it came down to putting them on a piece of paper and making a story . . . they fitted theirs into a story. . . . It's bit like giving a traumatised child a doll and the doll speaks because these clay figures . . . it was the man with a gun and a man in a boat . . . and it was interesting because we had this football game and this incredibly heart-wrenching scene with the communists and the government . . . and he's going to kill a man. . . . And the fact that they picked up the idea . . . the germ of the story when that first character went down and they were able to then take whatever they had made and put it into that story . . . showed something that I had never seen in them before . . . and I don't know quite what word I would say. . . . It showed that they were thinking of the narrative of the whole text and then putting in their element into the text . . . and some better than others . . . but they all contributed to it.

For the facilitator team and the participants there were a number of critical moments like this in the workshops. But certainly the box exercises and the integrated clay workshops seemed to construct moments of acute focus and reflection, creating small moments in which affective expression combined with emotional connection and language learning. These were particularly successful with sequences that included a form of visual/auditory art (box collage work, self-portraits, clay work, music and poetry/rap activities). These art activities were embedded within a sequence that followed a particular pattern: an imaginative and playful space created through drama games and activities (which created safety, generated trust and an energy of possibility that provided permission for risk taking); contextualized language scaffolding that was collaboratively produced or discovered and displayed on word walls (which provided the tools for greater extension with expression) or generated directly from doing; an arts-based activity that was introduced and enabled participants to work individually using the materials offered to experiment creatively through collage work, clay sculptures and poetry (that allowed for quiet introspective reflection and a chance to experiment with personal symbols, metaphors and a chance to rehearse and customize language); a sequence that culminated in a performative sharing – performing the rap in a circle of cheering classmates, displaying and explaining the artworks as if participating in a gallery exhibition tour, creating a group scene using individually formed representation of people, animals and other forms made of clay – to the whole group (which led to both increased confidence and language practice).

Emotion and connection

It was intriguing to see how the multi-arts practice developed from the pilot study to the second phase. To our minds there has been a refining and more careful integration between art forms. The exercises and activities link in a very direct way. The needs of the teacher and opportunities for enhancing and structuring language and vocabulary have been built in with greater degrees of integrity. One of the unpredictable themes to emerge from the process has been the importance of emotions. Throughout the case study projects we observed, made connections and drew significance on quite dramatic shifts in affective states among participants. Our analysis links the experience of three distinct emotional states with the potential of this art-based intervention to impact positively on well-being and resilience, language acquisition and the development of social connections between classmates. The remainder of the chapter explores the significance of these relationships between emotions, arts-based activities and learning.

From the beginning the drama work created energy and momentum. Each week, we introduced novel activities, or variations on a familiar theme, with theatre games, improvisations and body work that got participants out of their chairs (sometimes reluctantly to begin with) and engaged them in processes that were interactive, imaginative, playful, competitive. Theatre games involving team strategy and or competition evoked energy and enthusiasm, and our analysis of the photographs and videos, along with field notes and teacher reflections, indicate that theatre games of this nature provoked a shift in mood. At different points in the programme we observed in these students a state of playful engagement, a state of being wholly present and immersed. Photographs and videos taken during theatre games captured expressions, gestures, laughter and a level of physical energy that evidenced the pleasure and complicity that was evoked. The young people here were clearly responding to the opportunity to suspend the more adult and high stakes concerns they carried about achievement, security and material success, and take pleasure in the immediacy of an imaginative, high-energy game.

The significance of these moments of heightened enjoyment and playful engagement makes sense in the context of wider observations and reflections on emotions and mood and the connections to learning for this cohort. One of the earliest observations, while certainly not a clinical one, connects with the widely documented psychological repercussions of trauma (Alayarian 2007). Our observation was that many of these students were prone to a kind of despondency, an apathy or inertia that manifested in what we subjectively described as a kind of disassociation, as if they were removed for periods of time from their environment, separated by what we described as a 'membrane'. In addition to findings about the psychological and neurological effects of trauma and the implications of these for learning (Stemac et al. 2013), various other explanations for such apathy can been found in the research addressing different stages of the asylum seeking and resettlement process. Studies have shown that the period of time spent in a detention centre induces passivity (Horghagen and Josephsson 2010) and that a medicalized style of settlement support can induce new arrivals to adopt a passive and dependent approach to the process of resettling (Peisker and Tilbury 2003).

Another explanation for moments of reserve and lack of engagement may be feelings of ambivalence about the value of the work. While the young people consistently rated their satisfaction levels as high when oral and written feedback was sought, comments from the teacher indicated that confusion about the purpose of the work may have influenced their commitment at some points. This is hardly surprising given the well-documented issues with learning style incompatibility (Onsando and Billett 2009) that is frequently cited as an issue for new arrivals as they encounter the Australian education system. The imperative to achieve functional English as quickly as possible and the intense pressure these young people are under to progress quickly in acquiring English language skills is an overriding concern. This would conceivably mean that where the direct link to tangible outcomes was not immediately apparent, their involvement in (even enjoyable) learning activities was a luxury that they could ill-afford. The structural impediment to a more genuinely collaborative and synergistic approach to planning and follow-up activities in the classroom was recognized by teachers and researchers as a factor effecting the students' experience.

The third emotional state that was observed was one of heightened anxiety. The students in this programme often reported feeling highly anxious and their artwork reinforced the degree to which worry and stress affected them. Our case study supports other research which connects the prevalence of such high anxiety in this cohort with the high stakes attached to success in language and academic performance, the ambition to achieve educational qualifications that will lead to employment and the ensuing tangible outcomes in terms of security and identity (Moore et al. 2008). Many of these young people carry the burden of dependent families and communities in dangerous or untenable situations overseas, who also have a high hope and significant investments in their academic progress and material success in Australia.

As facilitators of this creative process we struggled at times with the unpredictable flows between these states. At several points we speculated on the causes of slumps in energy levels and the low mood of the group, and individuals within the group, and there was plenty of substance to draw upon in this respect. While shifts in the group dynamics were clearly influenced by fluctuations in group membership, the students frequently showed signs of distress and the nature of some of these anxieties was expressed through the drama and art work. These students had multiple worries, including anxiety about life situations and their futures (especially in terms of work), struggles with poverty, housing problems, discrimination, concern about family and community members not in Australia, upcoming assessment, along with clear indications of physical and mental ill health, such as complaints of headaches, sleeping problems, nightmares, back pain and so on. The class teacher reported that 'constantly changing energy levels is something all teachers are struggling with'.

For part of the project we had the support of a photographer/film-maker, a recently arrived refugee from Iran. His comment in a debrief session 6 weeks into the programme was that 'they're not happy' which stopped us in our tracks. He was observing a predisposition in the group, a sadness that seemed to sap energy from many of the participants. It was an observation that alerted us to our responsibility to respond to the ups and downs of the moods in the workshop. A recent study in the United Kingdom (Kohli 2006) which focused on social work practice with unaccompanied asylum seeking and refugee young people, unpacks some of the complexities of engaging with this group, and the need for a light, empathetic and compassionate touch. This study, based on a literature review and interviews examining 'how well the social workers knew the young people, particularly in terms of their past lives, in the context of silence and mistrust' (p. 713), found that

> silence is a complex phenomenon in relation to children and forced migration, and perhaps to all vulnerable children growing up in

uncertain circumstances. (The literature) appears to show that the maintenance of silence can both constrict and defend particular positions that unaccompanied minors adopt at particular times along their journeys of resettlement . . . they appeared to weigh up the costs and benefits of silence, alongside a rearrangement of stories of victimhood and endurance. (The social workers) described unaccompanied minors at various stages of moving from a contingent existence within their new lives to more solid foundations within which thicker stories could be safely told, so long as someone understood how and why they were sometimes silent. As practical helpers, as therapeutically minded listeners and as companionable people, they appeared to know the language of silence, and to respond well to the spoken and unspoken worlds that the children carried with them in their search for asylum. (p. 720)

In this project, drama and art-based practices offered an alternative to the 'language of silence'. It offered an opportunity to explore an as yet unspoken world, but we found the invitation to enter this world with us needed to come via play and pleasure. At this point we understood the imperative to make the work pleasurable. It was a turning point in our understanding of what might work. Field notes record this observation: 'we need to work for presence – smiles, non-verbal communication. We need to work against boredom – glazed eyes, passivity. The smile quota needs to be high in each class.'

The effect of negative emotions has received a lot of attention in language learning theory; anxiety may well be the most studied emotion in second language acquisition (MacIntyre and Gregersen 2012). Language anxiety trigger patterns of behaviour such as avoidance or escape not conducive to the level of risk and experimentation that learning a new language requires. As MacIntyre and Gregersen (2012) observe, however, that although it has received little attention from researchers in the past, recent developments in the literature have begun to highlight the power of positive emotions. They refer to Fredickson's (2006) 'broaden and build' theory that suggests that positive emotions function in at least five powerful ways relevant to learning a new language:

> First, positive emotions tend to broaden people's attention and thinking, leading to exploration and play, new experiences and new learning. Second, positive emotion helps to undo the lingering effects of negative emotional arousal. A related, third function of positive emotion is to promote resilience by triggering productive reactions to stressful events, such as improving cardiovascular recovery and making salient feelings of happiness and interest while under stress. Fourth, positive emotion promotes building personal resources, such as social bonds built by smiles, intellectual resources honed during creative play. . . . Fifth, positive emotions can be part of an upward spiral toward greater well being in the future, essentially the vicious cycle in reverse. A positive spiral is possible because the acquisition of resources facilitated by positive emotions endure long after the emotional reaction has ended. (p. 197)

As the programme progressed we began to document how the drama and art work was providing a performative context for an unsteady, stuttering and tentative pathway through the emotional turmoil of transition, growth and learning. For these young people with their powerful orientation to the future, their well-being is dependent on their capacity to negotiate a series of complex transitions. The importance of transformative learning theory was the focus of a recent study of the experiences of African students from refugee backgrounds in this Vocational Educational and Training context (Onsando and Billett 2009). As a whole the sequencing of composite elements in this drama and creative arts programme opened up pathways to transformative learning experiences via the powerful effects of emotions and imagination.

The link between emotional states, learning and aesthetics was a vital one in this project. Blanchard and Sowel (2005) in a paper discussing the transformative power of poetry explain that 'what makes artistic emotion different from the emotions we experiences daily is that it has been transformed . . . by way of imagination, symbolic language and a kind of abstraction (by which all extraneous elements are chipped away or burned off), the raw emotion is transformed into . . . significant form' (p. 253). These practitioner and teachers of poetry as a therapeutic art form analyse the link between emotion and rhythm drawing on philosophy, neuroscience and poetry. They claim that

> each emotion has its own sound, particular key, and unique rhythm. We also know from experience that when we fully undergo an emotion, it may then turn into another emotion . . . the passage from one emotion to another is the plot or the motion of an action, a wave, an impulse a sound that, with skill, can become a poem or a story, offering deep meaning. Transformation of emotion therefore, depends a great deal on rhythm and translation of this transformation depends a great deal on our poetic understanding of rhythm. (p. 252)

The ebb and flow of energy, stories, emotions, engagement and learning was rhythm in this project that could not be forced or monitored, assessed or measured. It moved to an unsteady, faltering beat, but the impulse to learn, adapt, imagine, create and survive passed like sand through the hands of the participants.

Penny's Research Journal

> The final moment, passing the sand, remembering favourite moments, gently ended the cycle. This exercise, repeated only twice in the process, remained fresh and I sensed that the answers in the main were not coerced . . . they came from an honest place, not 'what they think we want to hear'.

Research has repeatedly established the intense need of new arrivals in this cohort to connect with their peers, and the significant advantages that this may bring to their language learning experiences. They clearly have a lot to gain from the chance to build new relationships that will continue to sustain them beyond their relatively short time engaged in state sponsored settlement support. Given also the transient nature of their contact with each other, drama and multi-arts create an effective means of fast tracking the creation of positive social connections. In a more immediate sense, drama and multi-arts offer momentary but critical relief from the acute stresses and strains that young people from refugee backgrounds experience in these early stages of resettlement. It has potential to be an approach that works effectively against the 'affective barrier' that inhibits language acquisition.

The project worked to facilitate symbolic transitions by introducing different kinds of art-based activities that wove in and out of the work, creating a conversational, iterative dynamic. At times these articulations stretched participants and facilitators alike into spaces of discovery and risk-taking. At these points in the programme, we were all afforded – teachers, students and researchers alike – even just for brief moments, glimpses of new surprising possibilities, performances that took playful forays into a new territory of language use, rehearsed a new level of confidence and took the reconstructed identities and imagined communities that held these possibilities for a test run.

7

Conclusion – Living with Hope

I may be the amber light
but amber is the only gemstone that is a living
flowing, liquid – permanently fossilized
that keeps itself warm
that is used as medicine
that smells sweet when it gets burnt
that in Roman times was worth more than a slave
that was used to decorate Mycenaean tombs
that was named 'Ἠλέχτqο' by the Greeks
a precursor to the English word for 'electricity'
because they discovered that if it rubbed the wrong way
amber will always create a spark

Extract from Amber Lights by Luka Lesson (2013).

Once again Lesson uses the metaphor of amber to describe the in-between, hyphenated identity of migrant and refugee experience, but this time he extends the metaphor to remind us that amber is also a gem that can offer possibilities. The poem articulates amber as ancient, healing, priceless and the spark that can create light in a dark world. Amber is no longer being considered a negative aspect of refugee experience and Lesson now celebrates the amber state as one that is essentially hopeful and rich in potential.

Across this project, we have witnessed both aspects of the amber space as we worked with our young participants. We saw them struggle with the challenges of being betwixt and between cultures, attempting to effectively negotiate the settlement process while simultaneously navigating the ordinary challenges of growing up. However, we have also been fortunate witnesses to their resilience and hopefulness, understanding through our engagement with them, the rich potential of these new arrivals.

Our starting point for the research, supported by the literature and the grounded experience of the individuals and groups we worked with in Logan, was the idea that the first 2 years of settlement are critical in constructing successful long-term transitions into a new culture. Our partnership with MultiLink served to inform us, nourish our ideas and challenge our developing processes. Almost immediately, our understanding of resettlement and acculturation across the age groups shifted and we realized that we needed to focus in on the concrete here-and-now needs of individuals and groups, particularly language skills. However, there was also a hope that aspects of our work would extend beyond the concrete to deepen the processes of belonging, enable greater control over situations, develop additional skills and enhance confidence in undertaking positive challenges (Sarig 2001).

Our goals were linked to the concepts of resilience in the resettlement process, and we drew on several pieces of literature to support our understanding of them. For example, the impressive international, cross-cultural study of Ungar et al. (2007) was particularly useful, identifying seven tensions for young people dealing with the risks and adjustment factors of settlement. These tensions were conceived of as being dynamic and convergent in different ways across time and include:

- access to material resources (availability of financial, educational, medical and employment assistance and/or opportunities, as well as access to food, clothing and shelter);
- relationships (with significant others);
- identity (personal and collective sense of purpose, self-appraisal of strengths and weaknesses, aspirations, beliefs and values, including spiritual and religious identification);
- power and control (experiences of caring for one's self and others, the ability to affect change);
- cultural adherence (connection to local and global practices, values and beliefs);

- social justice (experiences related to finding a meaningful role in community);
- cohesion (feeling a part of something larger than one's self socially and/or spiritually).

We found these 'tensions' useful as a way of cross-referencing with the processes of creative participatory group work, suggesting very particular ways in which drama and the arts might benefit individuals and groups: to reinforce agency (power and control) in the learning process; enhance relationships (with peers, and significant others); help participants to explore notions of identity; and develop a sense of cohesion; or a stronger understanding of social justice by adopting new and additional roles and perspectives.

In this chapter, we draw on some of these ideas and others within the literature, together with key aspects of our collective experiences over the last few years, to identify the particular insights we have gained. Looking back though, it's fair to begin by saying that we are only now just beginning to realize where we should have started. Perhaps more precisely we realize that our understanding of the participants we worked with was limited – that across all of the case studies our ability to directly engage with, or fully understand, the resettlement journey of individuals and groups was restricted by time and the nature of our projects. Each case study was minimal in terms of the contribution it made to the existing work of each institutional environment, and while we all worked hard to integrate and add value to this daily work, the revelations and insights into the process of settlement we gained through our participation were necessarily momentary and partial.

Fortunately, the action of writing this book has driven us to question, argue and reflect on what we *have* learnt, to offer a number of insights about where the possible value of the three projects lay, and how they might provide hints for further practice. We hope that it is this acceptance of an unknowing state that provides both the possibility and the potential for co-creating work in the future. We begin this process by re-examining our understanding of the notion of resettlement.

Resettlement

Applied theatre practice, like any cultural work, is part of a broad and complex sociopolitical ecology. These ecologies are not always benign and are rarely stable. For the young people who arrive in their settlement country with potential and enthusiasm, the quality of their settlement will be keenly influenced by how they are received, both within their own refugee community and the wider community.

In the context of this research project, the ecology facing these new arrivals was itself in a state of transition, for in October 2013, a Federal election was held in Australia, bringing to power a new Liberal government and new Immigration Minister, Scott Morrison. Immediately he issued a missive to civil servants requiring them to change the bureaucratic name of asylum seekers who arrive by boat from 'Irregular Maritime Arrivals' to 'Illegal Maritime Arrivals', arguing that he was simply calling 'a spade a spade' (*The Guardian*, 21 October 2013).

Such political manoeuvres and bureaucratic terminologies seep into the public consciousness, potentially demonizing asylum seekers as illegal and positioning them as criminals. These neo-liberal and hard-line politics impact on the perceptions, policies and practices in tangible and intangible ways. The tentacles of bureaucratic re-positioning reach far and deep contaminating the environment of settlement. They must therefore be taken into account and considered carefully in any discussion of settlement.

Equally important is consideration of the cultural specificity of settlement and the differences that exist in relation to how transition and settlement is influenced by cultural paradigms. Given that our participants were individuals from Sudan, Congo, Rwanda, Afghanistan, Iran, Burundi, Eritrea, Myanmar (Burma), Laos, El Salvador, Macedonia and Thailand, consideration of this diversity was essential, for ideological values, family and community role expectations, behavioural practices and economical and environmental factors differ markedly from one of these cultural groups to the next.

Together then, these two aspects of an individual's world are critical to their settlement process for as Papadopoulos (2007, p. 310) points out:

[w]ider community and cultural contexts are not abstract terms but matter a great deal as they are active in forming at least part of the meaning systems of each individual. In difficult situations and adverse circumstances, the collective meaning tends to influence the individuals' value system much more than individuals are aware of.

For this reason, it now seems apparent to us that one of the missed opportunities of our research and hence our understanding of resettlement was a failure to connect more substantially with these two dimensions of ecology, and in particular with the elders and leaders of specific cultural communities. Such connections might have enabled us to build new networks and to create new ecological pathways for our work. Had we done so, our projects might have been more effective and more sustainable.

In spite of this shortcoming, we nevertheless learnt a good deal about the challenges inherent within the settlement process, especially for our older participants. For example, in the secondary school group the peer pressure and bullying scenarios, both from within and outside of the school, were clearly points of conflict and tension. Here the need for adolescents to belong to peer groups and gangs was evident, as were the tensions with traditional cultural beliefs that pulled them to separate from their elders in favour of the new cultural paradigm. To some degree these teenage participants might be conceived of as integrating better to the host culture, but at the same time the diluting of a bi-cultural identity, or the ability to live with the contradictions of the amber light, might bring them into tension with cultural adherence. The rejection of one culture for the acceptance of another is a form of denial, but perhaps this is part of an inevitable settlement journey. For some of the participants in the TAFE project, several of whom were unaccompanied minors, there were pressures to acclimatize quickly so that they could send money back to extended family members in other countries. This pressure manifested itself in a deep frustration with the time it takes to learn a language, get a job and get settled. For some of the participants there was some identification that this frustration was internalized, and that resulted in low self-confidence and a feeling of having little control over their circumstances.

These factors cannot be underestimated when considering settlement in its broadest sense, or indeed in terms of how drama and other arts-based approaches served to support it. Neither can they be underestimated in relation to the impact they have on resilience – the next focus for discussion.

Resilience

One of the starting points of our research was the concept of resilience and it is therefore interesting to note here that across the duration of the research our understanding of this concept shifted markedly. We began with the goal of developing or building the resilience of individuals, but in time came to understand that resilience for individuals is dependent upon context, and that rather than being a fixed personal characteristic of individuals, it is instead a fragile and complex characteristic that is more likely to be revealed through action than developed by it. This change in our inflection reflects the changing discourse within the literature in relation to this concept, where a similar shift away from constructing resilience as a personal trait to embracing more complex perspectives that articulate it as a dynamic process that is contingent and interconnected with the social ecology has emerged.

With this shift came a review in the function of the creative work, with a new emphasis being placed on identifying ways to resource resilience rather than construct it – to extend the range of contexts where individuals might feel positive and capable. Significantly, within the formal learning institutions we worked within, the young people were generally positive, expressing gratitude (for being in Australia) and a sense of hope for the future. At these times it seems that they felt comfortable within the relatively 'safe spaces' afforded them through the institutions we worked with. However, a number of the stories shared already in these pages, and those not included, reveal that in the world beyond these classrooms, strong pressures exert themselves on these young people – pressures that are exacerbated by tiredness, boredom, a sense of being overwhelmed by the difficulties with acculturation and bureaucracy.

Mostly though, there was hope – many different kinds of hope. Hope had different textures and intensities. For example, some of the unaccompanied participants described their experience in offshore detention camps as positive, with high levels of resources and quality teaching. Others highlighted hope within the 'honeymoon' phase of having recently been accepted into Australia, and what that promise might mean, bringing with it genuine gratitude and positive energy. Even in the post 'honeymoon' phase, hope was still present for many.

This tangible presence of hope in the groups we worked with also brought us to question the way we were thinking about resilience and caused us to return to Barber and Doty's (2013) work. This work challenges the viability of the construct of resilience by suggesting that the literature on conflict and youth tests it by showing that most young people adapt effectively. Again here we have to be careful to acknowledge the limited scope of our research, but it did seem that the young people we worked with appeared to adapt and reconstruct their lives in a way that refutes the logic of some aspects of the resilience framework and bringing into question the notion that resilience is something that an 'intervention' might establish or construct.

Perhaps the study of Lenette et al. (2012) on newly arrived, single women in Australia suggests a better way to position resilience in relation to understanding the resettlement process. In this work resilience is seen as part of the everyday routine of each day and over time. The authors argue that 'the everyday is not simply a vessel in which lives are lived, rather it is the milieu in which the social processes of resilience are enacted daily' (p. 639). Resilience and hope are then not heroic strategies that can be put in place by skilled practitioners, but rather mundane, fragile and quiet processes embodied in each individual and environment. They are processes of ingenuity and survival, performed moment by moment with the resources that are at hand.

If this is the case, what then did our dramatic and creative approaches offer? What contribution to the settlement process did our work make?

Drama

Over the 6 years we have partnered with MultiLink we have used a wide range of drama and theatre forms. Initially we started with a simple Forum Theatre project where very new arrivals were given the chance to learn from the experiences of more settled individuals. We then developed a project working with refugee actors that toured to schools focused on positive and surprising stories of settlement. There was also more process-driven work that aimed to support refugees in understanding Australian history so that they could pass the Citizen-ship test more easily. These early projects attempted to combine con-cern for the role of aesthetic engagement with instrumental learning outcomes.

In the three case studies reported in detail here, the weave of the aesthetic with concrete learning outcomes was also a potent feature, with language learning being the most important of the targeted goals. We therefore begin by examining the contribution drama made to language learning in this project, before moving on to identify key characteristics including agency, the exploration of identity and the building of relationships.

Drama and language

Across all of the projects, English language acquisition was clearly supported through and by the approaches we adopted. We make no quantitative claims here about the extent of this support, however, the descriptions of practice outlined in the earlier chapters indicate quite strongly that drama offers useful alternate ways of approaching and supporting the language learning needs of young people from refugee backgrounds. These approaches, which encourage playfulness and real ownership of language, within authentic contexts and for real purposes, are quite different from those more usually employed.

Of particular importance are the opportunities offered through dramatic activity to explore different registers, vocabulary and styles of language practice. For example, in the primary school case study the participants responded to the various facilitator roles, asking questions and offering advice to the characters, while in the secondary school case study the participants actively took on a range of roles as they attempted to resolve incidents of conflict and bullying, practising language skills in scenes that they had created.

In the primary school there were also considerable opportunities for children to apply vocabulary in order to advance and develop the co-constructed imaginative worlds of the drama. Here the motivation to use and expand on language was driven by deep engagement with the narratives being explored. As such, our research builds on the work of Belliveau and Kim (2014) who did an extensive analysis of the current literature about participatory drama projects in L2 contexts. It also supports the claims that they report about the way in which drama and arts activities invite participants to spontaneously interact in meaningful ways.

However, language teachers can sometimes find improvisation and drama approaches quite threatening. This is because within improvised learning contexts considerable ceding of control of the learning environment is required, and often L2 teachers have limited experiences of teaching in this mode. In our case studies this reluctance was evident, for while teachers were eager to observe and participate on the edges, they expressed a lack of confidence in their skills of being able to teach in this way. Our understanding is that the drama work enabled us to hand the power and agency to the learners in these contexts and this in turn significantly impacted on their engagement and learning.

Further research into the use of drama to support the language learning needs of newly arrived refugees is now needed. Such studies might help to identify, more specifically, how and why drama motivates language learning and the extent to which the contextualized and meaningful ways it is used to extend language skills impact upon achievement and motivation. In school and other educational contexts driven increasingly by benchmarking and a culture of performativity, and where approaches are too often functional and limited in order to address these pressures, drama and other arts-based practices have the potential to shift and enhance the outcomes for all young people, but especially those for whom motivation levels may be low.

Agency

A further area of learning derived from the three case studies was how the participatory approaches used within this study encouraged learner agency, with all three case studies aiming to adopt a more student-centred approach. Here the drama work integrated within these ecological structures to create microclimates that provided alternate, more playful spaces. These alternate spaces privileged the role of agency and the individual's potential for taking greater control over their learning. This emphasis on greater learner agency is not meant as a criticism of the educational institutions we partnered with, but rather is highlighted because it relates directly to the needs of newly arrived participants who, as Ungar et al. (2007) suggest, need opportunities to gain a sense of power and control, and to understand that they have the ability to affect changes in their lives.

One specific way the drama case studies attempted to enhance this agency was that across the workshops, participants were given a strong say in how content, stories and learning were articulated and performed. The result was a growing confidence in communicating and playing with different roles and an increased experience of being directly involved in the learning process. Across the three case studies there was also a strong sense of ownership in the process, with decisions being left for individuals and/or subgroups to make in different ways. These forms of engagement hopefully contributed to each individual experiencing a sense of the process interacting with their needs in direct ways, as opposed to learning being an abstract form of knowledge processing.

Perhaps this approach to learning also connects back to Levinas' concept of an ethical encounter with the other as being a form of *saying* rather than *said*, to create an encounter that is tentative and exploratory and part of a process of developing a greater sense of community among participants. Winston's (2013) notion is useful here in that he suggests that it is this form of dialogue and participation that supports the development of 'vocabularies of pleasure, hope, passion, emotion, experience and togetherness' (p. 135), while Neelands and Nelson (2013) argue that the drama encounter is an ethical one that encourages and fosters particular qualities of behaviour, including co-operation, altruism, trust and empathy.

Exploring identities

Goodman's (2004) study of how unaccompanied young people from Sudan transition to a new culture highlights the importance of processes that facilitate and support identity negotiation and making meaning of new lives:

> Listening to refugees' beliefs and about how they make sense of their experiences provided insight into how they managed difficulties and how they ordered their world. Such insight can be used to support them in their efforts for a better life (p. 1193).

In each context and within each approach, the possibilities for exploring notions of identity and meaning making were different but nevertheless present and significant. Within the primary school project, for example, the use of role by both the children and teachers, and the opportunities this provided to shift the status dynamics normally present in the classroom, afforded rich opportunities for new identities and relationships to be explored. Similarly, in the secondary classroom, the students, through their improvisations and the Forum theatre work, were able to test out new ways of dealing with power, conflict, respect and control or the lack of it. Finally, in the TAFE project, engagement with multiple art forms offered these sometimes very troubled young people, new ways to view learning and themselves as learners. Regardless then of age or context, the students quickly learnt to use drama to experiment with fictional situations that were meaningful to them, and increasingly they were able to construct imaginative and creative solutions that were effective in resolving problems, issues and experiences in their dramas.

As such, the various projects described within this book provided the participants with access to imaginative worlds that allowed them to temporarily step away from the stresses of adaptation in order to experience and play with, alternative identities in the fictional situations they created. Cooperative engagement in drama also enabled the students to be part of a community with a shared, common purpose.

Linked to the exploration of identity was the ways in which this work generated different forms of affective engagement. The emotional responses to the work ranged from joy and laughter to moments of deeper responses. Some of these emotions were created in response to the fictional worlds of the drama work, while others were directly connected to these young people's real-life experiences and their responses to them. While we were determined to create emotionally safe but nevertheless challenging, motivating and engaging learning spaces, avoiding trauma stories wherever possible, these newly arrived individuals regularly brought these to the work and surfaced them intentionally. In doing this, the participants revealed a degree of trust in our approach – feeling safe to share and explore, making connections of relevance and willingly sharing them. This suggests that across all of our projects, the drama classroom offered these new arrivals a safe space where connections between the past and present, as well as between individuals, cultures, genders and roles, were made possible. Barriers and membranes that can so easily divide young people seemed to be, for some individuals and in some circumstances, permeable when working through drama.

Relationships

Perhaps a common feature across the case studies was the ways in which the work created different approaches to classroom relationships. In the TAFE project for example, before the project most students did not know each other's names, and only talked with specific subgroups. However, in the course of the drama work students came to know each other better, sang songs, created work, watched each other perform and listened to each other's poetry. The benefit of this way of working was that the class relationships developed with much stronger bonds of connection and support. The teacher reported that participants had set up out-of-class support groups, and there had been an increase in social activities. Given the trend towards isolation, the introduction of this mode of teaching may have contributed to increased social connection. Indeed all the case studies worked to add social benefit by enhancing the capacity of participants to build relationships with their peers. In the secondary case study the participants worked with a range of different peer groups across ages, ethnicity and gender and was one of the important features of the process. This also occurred in the primary school where different groupings within the drama broke down previous social barriers. This is a particularly important element across the three case studies as in all cases the peer group were going through similar processes of settlement and transition, and therefore the group processes demanded by drama and other arts-based approaches enabled a greater degree of understanding and awareness.

Initially, especially within the TAFE project, there was some resistance to practices that seemed to have no specific purpose or learning aim, however, once group cohesion developed, many of these frustrations ebbed away. This was especially the case when the connection between learning, collaboration and creativity could be seen.

One of our key learning points then was the importance of making explicit and articulating clearly the rationale for our approaches, including identification of how our exercises might link to language learning. This issue was dealt with more effectively in the primary and secondary case studies where it was made clear that the drama facilitators were working to help the students achieve specific goals, and as a result they willingly entered into the work.

Towards hope

When we embarked on this research we hoped that our work might achieve some positive outcomes. In particular, we hoped that we might, in some small way, support the settlement journeys of the young people we worked with, while also identifying those approaches most appropriate for achieving these goals.

Our participants also had hopes and we slowly learnt about them. For example, one of the participants in the first cycle of the TAFE project always excused himself 30 minutes before the end of the lesson. After the second week, we checked in with the teacher, and she told us that he worked two jobs while also holding down his studies. He worked from midday to 7 p.m. at a fast food restaurant, and then from 9 p.m. until 4 in the morning in a meat factory. He slept for 4 hours and then came to college at 8 in the morning. Despite this he was alive with curiosity and determination, a bright and engaged student, always helping others in the class. The TAFE teacher described his long journey from his first 'honeymoon' period full of optimism, leading towards a gradual disintegration and frustration with how to transition and survive, and finally to a realistic pathway through further education, work and making contacts so that he would not have to work such long hours. He was very conscious of his transition journey, and described the process as 'living with hope – the right kind of hope'.

His story in many ways parallels ours. We too began with a sense of optimism, experienced some frustration, and finally transitioned to a more realistic understanding of the limitations but also possibilities of our approaches. These limitations acknowledge the challenges of life in the 'amber light' space and the constraints imposed by broader communities.

As we finish off the writing of this book we are about to embark on a new project working with young people from a range of asylum-seeker backgrounds – not all of whom have achieved a positive settlement status. We aim to keep on learning, playing and listening to the stories of these resilient young people, in the belief that drama and the arts might reveal, celebrate and enhance the 'right kind of hope'.

Bibliography

Ager, A. and Strang, A. (2008), 'Understanding integration: A conceptual framework', *Journal of Refugee Studies*, 21(2): 166–91.

Ahearn, F. L. (2000), *Psychosocial Wellness Of Refugees: Issues In Qualitative And Quantitative Research*, Oxford: Berghahn Books.

Ai, A., Tice, T. and Whitsett, D. (2007), 'Posttraumatic symptoms and growth of Kosovar war refugees: The influence of hope and cognitive coping', *The Journal of Positive Psychology*, 2(1): 55–65.

Alayarian, A. (2007), 'Trauma, resilience and creativity: Examining our therapeutic approach in working with refugees', *European Journal of Psychotherapy & Counselling*, 9(3): 313–24.

Allan, J. and Hess, L. (2010), 'The Nexus between material circumstances, cultural context and experiences of loss, grief and trauma: Complexities in working with refugees in the early phases of resettlement', *Social Science*, 13(3): 76–80.

Allwood, M., Bell-Dolan, D. and Husain, S. (2002), 'Children's trauma and adjustment reactions to violent and nonviolent war experiences', *Journal of the American Academy of Child & Adolescent Psychiatry*, 41(4): 450–7.

Anderson, M. and Dunn, J. (eds) (2013), *How Drama Activates Learning Contemporary Research and Practice*, London: Bloomsbury Academic.

Askland, H. (2005), 'Young Timorese in Australia: Becoming part of a new culture and the impact of refugee experiences on identity and belonging', unpublished dissertation, University of Newcastle, NSW.

Balfour, M. (ed.) (2013), *Refugee Performance: Practical Encounters*, Bristol: Intellect Books.

Barber, B. and Doty, S. (2013), 'How can a majority be resilient? Critiquing the utility of the construct of resilience through a focus on youth in contexts of political conflict', in J. Fernando and M. Ferrari (eds), *Handbook of Resilience in Children of War*, New York: Springer Science and Business Media, pp. 233–52.

Barnes, G. (2011), Report on the generation of the 2010 Index of Community
    Socio-Educational Advantage (ICSEA). http://www.acara.edu.au/verve/_
    resources/2010_Index_of_Community_Socio-Educational_Advantage_
    Generation_Report.pdf. Accessed, 10/1/14.

Batista-Pinto Wiese, E. (2010), 'Culture and migration: Psychological trauma
    in children and adolescents', *Traumatology*, 16(4): 142–52.

Beatty, J. (2009), *Creating a Shared Experience*. Retrieved from www.tesol.org.
    au/files/files/118_JaneBeatty.doc, 14 December 2011.

Beiser, M. (2009), 'Resettling refugees and safeguarding their mental health:
    Lessons learned from the Canadian Refugee Resettlement Project',
    Transcultural Psychiatry, 46(4): 539–83.

Belliveau, G. and Kim, W. (2014), 'Drama in L2 learning: A research synthesis',
    Scenario, vol. 2, accessed on line, unpaginated.

Berry, J. (2009), 'A critique of critical acculturation', *International Journal of
    Intercultural Relations*, 33(5): 361–71.

Berry, J. and Sam, D. (1997), 'Acculturation and adaptation', *Handbook of
    Cross-cultural Psychology*, 3(1): 291–326.

Berry, J., Phinney, J., Sam, D. and Vedder, P. (2006), 'Immigrant youth:
    Acculturation, identity, and adaptation', *Applied Psychology*, 55(3):
    303–32.

Betancourt, T. S. and Khan, K. T. (2008), 'The mental health of children
    affected by armed conflict: Protective processes and pathways to resilience',
    International Review of Psychiatry, 20(3): 317–28.

Bhabha, H. K. (1994), *The Location of Culture*, New York: Routledge.

Blanchard, M. M. and Sowbel, S. B. (2005), '"The breaking of waves in a steady
    surf": The transformative power of rhythm and emotion in poetry', *Journal
    of Poetry Therapy*, 18(1): 249–63.

Boal, A. (1979), *Theatre of the Oppressed*, New York: Theatre Communications
    Group.

Bolton, G. and Heathcote, D. (1998), 'Teaching culture through drama', in
    M. Byram and M. Fleming (eds), *Language Learning an Intercultural
    Perspective*, Cambridge: Cambridge University Press, pp. 118–30.

Bronfenbrenner, U. (1979), *The Ecology of Human Development*, Cambridge,
    MA: Harvard University Press.

Burton, B. (1991), *The Act of Learning: The Drama-Theatre Continuum in the Classroom*, Melbourne: Longman Cheshire.

—(2011), *Living Drama 4th Edition*, Melbourne: Pearson Education.

Burton, B. and O'Toole, J. (2009), 'Power in their hands: The outcomes of the Acting Against Bullying Research Project', *Applied Theatre Researcher*, 10: 1–15.

Burvill, T. (2008), '"Politics begins as ethics": Levinasian ethics and Australian performances concerning refugees', *Research in Drama Education: The Journal of Applied Theatre and Performance*, 13(2): 233–43.

Cahill, H. (2013), 'Drama for health and human relationships', in M. Anderson and J. Dunn (eds), *How Drama Activates Learning: Contemporary Research and Practice*, London: Bloomsbury, pp. 178–92.

Carini, R. M., Kuh, G. D. and Klein, S. P. (2006), 'Student engagement and student learning: Testing the linkages', *Research in Higher Education*, 47(1): 1–32.

Chappell, C. (1999), *Issues of Teacher Identity in a Restructuring VET System. RCVET Working Paper 99.31*. Available at: http://www.uts.edu.au/fac/edu/rcvet/working%20papers/9931Chap.pdf.

Chirkov, V. (2009), 'Critical psychology of acculturation: What do we study and how do we study it, when we investigate acculturation?' *International Journal of Intercultural Relations*, 33(2): 94–105.

Choudry, Aziz (2010) (book review), Dip Kapoor and Steven Jordan (eds) (2009), *Education, Participatory Action Research, and Social Change: International Perspectives*, New York: Palgrave Macmillan. *International Education*, 39(2). Retrieved from: http://trace.tennessee.edu/international education/vol39/iss2/6.

Clark, S. and Gilmour, J. (2011), 'Working with recently arrived horn of Africa youth: An intercultural partnership approach to community cultural development', *Culture and Local Governance*, 3(1): 59–70.

Clarke, A. E. (2003), 'Stiuational analysis: Grounded theory mapping after the postmodern turn', *Symbolic Interaction*, 26(4): 553–76.

Collie, P., Kindon, S., Liu, J. and Podsiadlowski, A. (2010), 'Mindful identity negotiations: The acculturation of young Assyrian women in New Zealand', *International Journal of Intercultural Relations*, 34(3): 208–20.

Conquergood, D. (2002), 'Performance studies: Interventions and radical research', *TDR/The Drama Review*, *46*(2): 145–56.

Correa-Velez, I., Gifford, S. and Barnett, A. (2010), 'Longing to belong: Social inclusion and wellbeing among youth with refugee backgrounds in the first three years in Melbourne, Australia', *Social Science and Medicine*, *71*(8): 1399–408.

Cranitch, M. (2011), 'Developing language and literacy skills to support refugee students in the transition from primary to secondary school', *Australian Journal of Language and Literacy*, *33*(3): 255–67.

Davidson, G., Murray, K. E. and Schweitzer, R. (2008), 'Review of refugee mental health and wellbeing: Australian perspectives', *Society*, *43*(3): 160–74.

Day, L. (2002), '"Putting yourself in other people's shoes": The use of forum theatre to explore refugee and homeless issues in schools', *Journal of Moral Education*, *31*(1): 21–34.

Dennis, R. (2008), 'Refugee performance: Aesthetic representation and accountability in playback theatre', *Research in Drama Education: The Journal of Applied Theatre and Performance*, *13*(2): 211–15.

Department of Immigration and Multicultural Affairs (2006), *Settlement Needs of New Arrivals*, Canberra: Commonwealth of Australia.

Doran, E. (2005), 'Working with Lebanese refugees in a community resilience model', *Community Development Journal*, *40*(2): 182–91.

Dunbar-Ortiz, R. and Harrell-Bond, B. E. (1987), 'Who protects the human rights of refugees?' *Africa Today*, 1.

Dunn, J. and Anderson, M. (2013), 'Drama and the future: Activating new possibilities', in M. Anderson and J. Dunn (eds), *How Drama Activates Learning: Contemporary Research and Practice*, London: Bloomsbury, pp. 293–306.

Dunn, J. and Stinson, M. (2012), 'Dramatic play and drama in the early years: Re-imagining the approach', in S. Wright (ed.), *Children, Meaning Making and the Arts* (2nd edn), French's Forest: Pearson, pp. 115–34.

Dunn, J., Bundy, P. and Woodrow, N. (2012), 'Combining drama pedagogy with digital technologies to support the language learning needs of newly arrived refugee children: A classroom case study', *RIDE: The Journal of Applied Theatre and Performance*, *17*(4): 477–99.

Eisenbruch, M., de Jong, J. T. V. M. and van de Put, W. (2004), 'Bringing order out of chaos: A culturally competent approach to managing the problems of refugees and victims of organized violence', *Journal of Traumatic Stress*, *17*(2): 123–31.

Ellis, B. H., Kia-Keating, M., Yusuf, S. A., Lincoln, A. and Nur, A. (2007), 'Ethical research in refugee communities and the use of community participatory methods', *Transcultural Psychiatry*, *44*(3): 459–81.

Engel, G. L. (1977), 'The need for a new medical model: A challenge for biomedicine', *Science*, *196*(4286): 129–36.

Faulkner, S. (2003), 'Asylum seekers, imagined geography and visual culture', *Visual Culture in Britain*, *4*(1): 93–144.

Fawzi, M. C., Pham, T., Lin, L., Nguyen, T. V., Ngo, D., Murphy, E. and Mollica, R. F. (1997), 'The validity of posttraumatic stress disorder among Vietnamese refugees', *Journal of Traumatic Stress*, *10*(1): 101–8.

Fazel, M., Wheeler, J. and Danesh, J. (2005), 'Prevalence of serious mental disorder in 7000 refugees resettled in western countries: A systematic review', *The Lancet*, *365*(9467): 1309–14.

Ferjoa, Tania and Margaret, Vickers (2010), 'Supporting refugee students in school education in Greater Western Sydney', *Critical Studies in Education, 51*(2): 149–62.

Fox, J. (2007), 'Playback theatre: Inciting dialogue and building community through personal story', *TDR/The Drama Review*, *51*(4): 89–105.

Fozdar, F. (2009), 'The "Golden Country": Ex-Yugoslav and African refugee experiences of settlement and "depression"', *Journal of Ethnic and Migration Studies, 35*(8): 1335–52.

Fozdar, F. and Hartley, L. (2013), 'Refugee resettlement in Australia: What we know and need to know', *Refugee Survey Quarterly*, *32*(3): 23–51.

Freire, P. (1998), *Pedagogy of Freedom: Ethics, Democracy, and Civic Courage*, London: Rowman & Littlefield.

Gagnon, A. J., Tuck, J. and Barkun, L. (2004), 'A systematic review of questionnaires measuring the health of resettling refugee women', *Health Care for Women International, 25*(2): 111–49.

Garbarino, J. and Bruyere, E. (2013), 'Resilience in the lives of children of war', in C. Fernando and M. Ferrari (eds), *Handbook of Resilience in Children of War*, New York: Springer, pp. 253–66.

Giddens, A. (1991), *Modernity and Self-Identity: Self and Society in the Modern Age*, Cambridge, MA: Polity Press.

Gifford, S. M., Bakopanos, C., Kaplan, I. and Correa-Velez, I. (2007), 'Meaning or measurement? Researching the social contexts of health and settlement among newly-arrived refugee youth in Melbourne, Australia', *Journal of Refugee Studies, 20*(3): 414–40.

Goodlad, S. and Hirst, B. (1989), *Peer Tutoring: A Guide to Learning by Teaching*, London: Kogan Page.

Goodman, J. H. (2004), 'Coping with trauma and hardship among unaccompanied refugee youths from Sudan', *Qualitative Health Research, 14*(9): 1177–96.

Gordon, E. E. (2005), *Peer Tutoring: A Teacher's Resource Guide*, Lanham, MD: Scarecrow Education.

Gozdziak, E. M. (2004), 'Training refugee mental health providers: Ethnography as a bridge to multicultural practice', *Human Organization, 63*(2): 203–10.

Gregory, D. and Urry, J. (eds) (1985), *Social Relations and Spatial Structures*, London: Macmillan.

Guardian, The (2013), 'Scott Morrison defends decision to call asylum seekers "illegal maritime arrivals"', 21 October 2013, http://www.theguardian.com/world/2013/oct/21/news-asylumseekers-immigration-government.

Hallahan, L. and Irizarry, C. (2008), 'Fun days out: Normalising social experiences for refugee children', *Journal of Family Studies, 14*: 124–30.

Harney, P. A. (2007), 'Resilience processes in context: Contributions and implications of Bronfenbrenner's person-process-context model', *Journal of Aggression, Maltreatment & Trauma, 14*(3): 73–87.

Harris, D. A. (2009), 'The paradox of expressing speechless terror: Ritual liminality in the creative arts therapies' treatment of posttraumatic distress', *The Arts in Psychotherapy, 36*(2): 94–104.

Haseman, B. and O'Toole, J. (1990), *Communicate Live!: Exploring the Functions of Spoken Language*, Port Melbourne, VIC: Heinemann Educational.

Hollifield, M., Warner, T. D., Lian, N., Krakow, B., Jenkins, J. H., Kesler, J. and Westermeyer, J. (2002), 'Measuring trauma and health status in refugees: A critical review', *The Journal of The American Medical Association, 288*(5): 611–21.

Horghagen, S. and Josephsson, S. (2010), 'Theatre as liberation, collaboration and relationship for asylum seekers', *Journal of Occupational Science, 17*(3) (October 2012): 37–41.

Hunter, M. A. (2008), 'Cultivating the art of safe space', *Research in Drama Education, 13*(1): 5–21.

Jackson, A. (2005), 'The dialogic and the aesthetic: Some reflections on theatre as a learning medium', *The Journal of Aesthetic Education, 39*(4): 104–18.

Jeffers, A. (2008), 'Dirty truth: Personal narrative, victimhood and participatory theatre work with people seeking asylum', *Research in Drama Education: The Journal of Applied Theatre and Performance, 13*(2): 217–21.

—(2012), *Refugees, Theatre and Crisis: Performing Global Identities*, Basingstoke: Palgrave MacMillan.

Johnson, B. and Down, B. (2013), 'Critically re-conceptualising early career teacher resilience', *Discourse: Studies in the Cultural Politics of Education, 34*(5): 703–15.

Jones, C. (2004), 'From healing rituals to music therapy: Bridging the cultural divide between therapist and young Sudanese refugees', *The Arts in Psychotherapy, 31*(2): 89–100.

Kao, S. M. and O'Neill, C. (1998), *Words into Worlds: Learning a Second Language through Process Drama*, Portsmouth, NH: Greenwood Publishing Group.

Kana, P. and Aitken, V. (2007), '"She didn't ask me about my grandma": Using process drama to explore issues of cultural exclusion and educational leadership', *Journal of Educational Administration, 45*(6): 697–710.

Kemmis, S. and McTaggart, R. (2005), 'Participatory action research: Communicative action and the public sphere', in N. Denzin and L. Lincoln (eds), *The Sage Handbook of Qualitative Research*, Thousand Oaks, CA: Sage, pp. 559–603.

Khawaja, N. G., White, K. M., Schweitzer, R. and Greenslade, J. (2008), 'Difficulties and coping strategies of Sudanese refugees: A qualitative approach', *Transcultural Psychiatry, 45*(3): 489–512.

Kim, S., Ehrich, J. and Ficorilli, L. (2012), 'Perceptions of settlement well-being, language proficiency, and employment: An investigation of immigrant adult language learners in Australia', *International Journal of Intercultural Relation, 36*(1): 41–52.

Kohli, R. K. S. (2006), 'The sound of silence: Listening to what unaccompanied asylum-seeking children say and do not say', *British Journal of Social Work, 36*(5): 707–21.

Kovacev, L. and Shute, R. (2004), 'Acculturation and social support in relation to psychosocial adjustment of adolescent refugees resettled in Australia', *International Journal of Behavioral Development, 28*(3): 259–67.

Kramsch, C. (2008), 'Ecological perspectives on Foreign Language education', *Language Teaching, 41*(3): 389.

Lenette, C., Brough, M. and Cox, L. (2012), 'Everyday resilience: Narratives of single refugee women with children', *Qualitative Social Work, 12*(5): 637–53.

Lesson, L. (2013), 'Amber Lights' in *The Future Ancients*, self published work.

Levinas, E. and Nemo, P. (1985), *Ethics and Infinity*, Pittsburgh, PA: Duquesne University Press.

Liebmann, Maria (2004), *Arts Approaches to Conflict*, London: Jessica Kingsley Publishers.

Liu, J. (2002), 'Process drama in second- and foreign-language classrooms', in Gerd Bräuer (ed.), *Body and Language. Intercultural Learning Through Drama*, Westport, CT and London: Ablex Publishing, pp. 1–25.

Lofgren, H. and Malm, B. (2005), *Bridging The fields of Drama and Conflict Management: Empowering Students to Handle Conflicts through School – Based Programmes*, Studia Psychologica et Paedagogica Series Altera CLXX, Malmo University Sweden, School of Teacher Education.

Logan City Council, 'Statistics and facts', http://www.logan.qld.gov.au/about-logan/living-in-logan/statistics-and-facts. Retrieved 3 February 2014.

Lynch, W. F. (1965), *Images of hope: Imagination as healer of the hopeless*, Baltimore: Helicon.

MacIntyre, P. D. and Gregersen, T. (2012), 'Emotions that facilitate language learning: The positive–broadening power of the imagination', *Studies in Second Language Learning and Teaching, 2*: 193–213.

Marlowe, J. M. (2010), 'Beyond the discourse of trauma: Shifting the focus on Sudanese refugees', *Journal of Refugee Studies, 23*(2): 183–98.

Matthews, J. (2008), 'Schooling and settlement: Refugee education in Australia', *International Studies of Sociology in Education, 18*(1): 31–45.

Mbago, P. (2011), 'Negotiating cultural identity through the arts: Fitting in, third space and cultural memory', *Journal of Arts & Communities, 3*(1): 89–104.

McPherson, M. (2010), '"I integrate, therefore I am": Contesting the normalizing discourse of integrationism through conversations with refugee women', *Journal of Refugee Studies, 23*(4): 546–70.

Mitchell, J., Kaplan, I. and Crowe, L. (2007), 'Two cultures: One life', *Community Development Journal, 42*(3): 282–98.

Moore, H., Nicholas, H. and Deblaquiere, J. (2008), *'Opening the Door': Provision for Refugee Youth with Minimal/No Schooling in the Adult Migrant English Program*, Sydney: Macquarie University and Department of Immigration and Citizenship.

Morrison, M., Burton, B. and O'Toole, J. (2006), 'Re-engagement through peer teaching drama – Insights into reflective practice', in P. Barnard and S. Hennessy (eds), *Reflective Practices in Arts Education*, Netherlands: Springer, pp. 139–48.

Multicultural Youth Advocacy Network (2012), *'Unaccompanied Minors in Australia. An Overview of National Support Arrangements and Key Emerging Issues'*, 304 Drummond Street, Carlton, Victoria 3053, Australia.

Murray, D. E. and Christison, M. (2011), *What English Language Teachers Need to Know. Volume II: Facilitating Learning*, London: Routledge.

Murray, D. E. and Lloyd, R. (2008), *Uptake of the special preparatory program by African communities: Attitudes and expectations*, Sydney: AMEP Research Centre.

Murray, K. E., Schweitzer, R. D. and Davidson, G. R. (2010), 'Review of refugee mental health assessment: Best practices and recommendations', *Journal of Pacific Rim Psychology, 4*(01): 72–85.

Neelands, J. (2009), 'Acting together: Ensemble as a democratic process in art and life', *Research in Drama Education: The Journal of Applied Theatre and Performance, 14*(2): 173–89.

Neelands, J. and Nelson, B. (2013), 'Drama, community and achievement: Together I'm someone', in M. Anderson and J. Dunn (eds), *How Drama Activates Learning: Contemporary Research and Practice*, London and New York: Bloomsbury, pp. 15–29.

Neuner, F. and Schauer, M. (2004), 'A comparison of narrative exposure therapy, supportive counseling, and psychoeducation for treating posttraumatic stress disorder in an African refugee settlement', *Journal of Consulting and Clinical Psychology, 72*(4): 579–87.

Nicholson, H. (2006), *Applied Drama: The Gift of Theatre*, Basingstoke: Palgrave Macmillan.

O'Connor, P. (2013), 'Drama as critical pedagogy: Re-imagining terrorism', in M. Anderson and J. Dunn (eds), *How Drama Activates Learning: Contemporary Research and Practice*, London: Bloomsbury, pp. 125–34.

O'Neill, C. (1995), *Drama Worlds: A Framework for Process Drama*, Portsmouth, NH: Heinemann.

O'Toole, J. (1991), *Oracy: The Forgotten Basic*, Brisbane: Ministers Consultative Committee on Curriculum.

O'Toole, J. and Dunn, J. (2002), *Pretending to Learn: Helping Children Learn Through Drama*, Sydney: Pearsons Australia (Longman).

O'Toole, J. and Stinson, M. (2013), 'Drama, speaking and listening: The treasure of oracy', in M. Anderson and J. Dunn (eds), *How Drama Activates Learning: Contemporary Research and Practice*, London and New York: Bloomsbury, pp. 159–77.

O'Toole, J., Burton, B. and Plunkett, A. (2005), *Cooling Conflict: A New Approach to Managing Bullying and Conflict in Schools*, Frenchs Forest, NSW: Pearson Education Australia.

Ollerhead, S. (2012), '"Passivity" or "potential"? Teacher responses to learner identity in the low-level adult ESL literacy classroom', *Literacy and Numeracy Studies, 20*(1): 63–84.

Onsando, G. and Billett, S. (2009), 'African students from refugee backgrounds in Australian TAFE institutes: A case for transformative learning goals and processes', *International Journal of Training Research,* 7(2): 80–94.

Papadopoulos, R. (2007), 'Refugees, trauma and adversity-activated development', *European Journal of Psychotherapy Counselling,* 9(3): 301–12.

Peisker, V. C. and Tilbury, F. (2003), '"Active" and "Passive" resettlement: The influence of support services and refugees' own resources on resettlement style', *International Migration,* 41(5): 61–91.

Porter, M. (2007), 'Global evidence for a biopsychosocial understanding of refugee adaptation', *Transcultural Psychiatry,* 44(3): 418–39.

Pufall, P. and Unsworth, R. (2004), 'Introduction: The imperative and the process for rethinking childhood', in P. Pufall and R. Unsworth (eds), *Rethinking Childhood,* New Jersey: Rutgers University Press, pp. 1–21.

Pupavac, V. (2008), 'Refugee advocacy, traumatic representations and political disenchantment', *Government and Opposition,* 43(2): 270–92.

Renzaho, A. M. N. and Vignjevic, S. (2011), 'The impact of a parenting intervention in Australia among migrants and refugees from Liberia, Sierra Leone, Congo, and Burundi: Results from the African Migrant Parenting Program', *Journal of Family Studies,* 17(1): 71–9.

Robinson, J. A. (2013), 'No place like home: Resilience among adolescent refugees resettled in Australia', in C. Fernando and M. Ferrari (eds), *Handbook of Resilience in Children of War,* New York: Springer, pp. 193–210.

Rosenberg, J., Gonzalez, M. J. and Rosenberg, S. (2005), 'Clinical practice with immigrants and refugees: An ethnographic multicultural approach', in E. Congress and M. J. Gonzalez (eds), *Multicultural Perspectives in Working with Families* (2nd edn), New York: Sheridan Books, pp. 259–79.

Rossiter, M. J. and Rossiter, K. R. (2009), 'Diamonds in the rough: Bridging gaps in supports for at-risk immigrant and refugee youth', *Journal of International Migration and Integration/Revue de l'integration et de la migration internationale,* 10(4): 409–29.

Rotas, A. (2004), 'Is "refugee art" possible?' *Third Text, 18*(1): 51–60.

Rothwell, J. (2012), 'Drama and languages education: Authentic assessment through process drama', *Second Language Learning through Drama*, 54–68.

Rubin J. and Herbert, M. (1998), *How to Plan and Implement a Peer-Coaching Program*, Richmond, VA: Association for Supervision and Curriculum Development.

Rudmin, F. W. (2010), 'Editorial: Steps towards the renovation of acculturation research paradigms: What scientists' personal experiences of migration might tell science', *Culture & Psychology, 16*(3): 299–312.

Salverson, J. (1999), 'Transgressive storytelling or an aesthetics of injury: Performance, pedagogy and ethics', *Theatre Research in Canada, 20*(1), available at http://journals.hil.unb.ca/index.php/tric/article/view/7096/8155 (no pagination).

—(2001), 'Change on whose terms? Testimony and an erotics of injury', *Theater, 31*(3): 119–25.

Sarig, A. (2001), 'Components of Community Resilience', *unpublished paper (Hebrew)*.

Schewe, M. L. (2002), 'Teaching foreign language literature: Tapping the students' bodily-kinaesthetic intelligence', in Gerd Bräuer (ed.), *Body and Language. Intercultural Learning through Drama*, Westport, CT and London: Able Publishing.

Schweitzer, R., Melville, F., Steel, Z. and Lacherez, P. (2006), 'Trauma, post-migration living difficulties, and social support as predictors of psychological adjustment in resettled Sudanese refugees', *Australian and New Zealand Journal of Psychiatry, 40*(2): 179–87.

Seddon, T. (2008), 'Crafting capacity in VET: Towards an agenda for learning and researching in the VET workforce', in *11th Annual Australian Vocational Education and Training Research Association Conference*, VET in Context. Available at: http://www.avetra.org.au/annual_conference/papers.shtml.

Silove, D. (1999), 'The psychosocial effects of torture, mass human rights violations, and refugee trauma: Toward an integrated conceptual framework', *The Journal of Nervous and Mental Disease, 187*(4): 200–7.

Silove, Derrick, Steel, Z., Bauman, A., Chey, T. and McFarlane, A. (2007), 'Trauma, PTSD and the longer-term mental health burden amongst Vietnamese refugees: A comparison with the Australian-born population', *Social Psychiatry and Psychiatric Epidemiology*, 42(6): 467–76.

Simich, L., Beiser, M. and Mawani, F. N. (2003), 'Social support and the significance of shared experience in refugee migration and resettlement', *Western Journal of Nursing Research*, 25(7): 872–91.

Sonderegger, R. and Barrett, P. M. (2004), 'Patterns of cultural adjustment among young migrants to Australia', *Journal of Child and Family Studies*, 13(3): 341–56.

Steel, Z., Silove, D., Phan, T. and Bauman, A. (2002), 'Long-term effect of psychological trauma on the mental health of Vietnamese refugees resettled in Australia: A population-based study', *The Lancet*, 360(9339): 1056–62.

Stepakoff, S. (2007), 'The healing power of symbolization in the aftermath of massive war atrocities: Examples from Liberian and Sierra Leonean survivors', *Journal of Humanistic Psychology*, 47(3): 400–12.

Stermac, L., Clarke, A. K. and Brown, L. (2013), 'Pathways to resilience: The role of education in war-zone immigrant and refugee student success', in C. Fernando and M. Ferrari (eds), *Handbook of Resilience in Children of War*, New York: Springer, pp. 211–20.

Stichick, T. and Bruderlein, C. (2001), *Children Facing Insecurity: New Strategies for Survival in a Global Era*, Policy paper produced for the Canadian Department of Foreign Affairs and International Trade, The Human Security Network, 3rd Ministerial Meeting, Petra, Jordan. 11–12 May 2001.

Stinson, M. and Freebody, K. (2006), 'The Dol project: The contributions of process drama to improved results in English oral communication', *Youth Theatre Journal*, 20(1): 27–41.

Stinson, M. and Piazzoli, E. (2013), 'Drama for additional language learning: Dramatic contexts and pedagogical possibilities', in M. Anderson and J. Dunn (eds), *How Drama Activates Learning: Contemporary Research and Practice*, London and New York: Bloomsbury, pp. 208–25.

Strawbridge, S. (2000), 'Some thoughts on connections between the political and the therapeutic in the work of Fox and Boal', *Dramatherapy*, 22(2): 8–12.

Taylor, J., Wilkinson, D. and Cheers, B. (2008), *Working With Communities: In Health and Human Services*, Oxford: Oxford University Press.

Taylor, Sandra (2008), 'Schooling and the settlement of refugee young people in Queensland: ". . . the challenges are massive"', *Social Alternatives, 27*(3): 58–65.

Terheggen, M. A., Stroebe, M. S. and Kleber, R. J. (2001), 'Western concept-ualizations and eastern experience: A cross-cultural study of traumatic stress reactions among Tibetan refugees in India', *Journal of Traumatic Stress, 14*: 391–403.

Thompson, J. (2011), 'Humanitarian performance and the Asian Tsunami', *TDR/The Drama Review, 55*(1): 70–83.

Thompson, J., Hughes, J. and Balfour, M. (2009), *Performance in Place of War*, London: Seagull.

To, D., Chan, Y., Lam, C. and Tsang, S. (2011), 'Reflections on a primary school teacher professional development programme on learning english through process drama', *Research in Drama Education: The Journal of Applied Theatre and Performance, 16*(4): 517–39.

Tran, T., Manalo, V. and Nguyen, V. (2007), 'Nonlinear relationship between length of residence and depression in a community-based sample of Vietnamese Americans', *International Journal of Social Psychiatry, 53*(1): 85–94.

Ungar, M., Brown, M., Liebenberg, L., Othman, R., Kwong, W. M., Armstrong, M. and Gilgun, J. (2007), 'Unique pathways to resilience across cultures', *Adolescence, 42*(166): 24.

United Nations, *Handbook on Procedures and Criteria for Determining Refugee Status under the 1951 Convention and the 1967 Protocol relating to the Status of Refugees* HCR/IP/4/Eng/REV.1 Reedited, Geneva, January 1992, UNHCR 1979. (See also the website of the Office of the United Nations High Commissioner for Refugees for other handbooks and guidelines: http://www.unhcr.org.)

UNHCR (2012), 2011 Statistical Yearbook, United Nations High Commissioner for Refugees (UNHCR). http://www.unhcr.org/statistics.

United States Holocaust Memorial Museum, 'Voyage of the St Louis', http://www.ushmm.org/wlc/en/article.php?ModuleId=10005267 [accessed 16 December 2013].

Wakholi, P. and Wright, P. (2011), 'The art of migrant lives. Bicultural identity and the arts: The African cultural memory youth arts festival in Western Australia', in C. L. McLean and R. Kelly (eds), *Creative Arts in Research for Community and Cultural Change*, Calgary, Alberta: Detselig Enterprises/Temeron Books. Accessed via http://researchrepository. murdoch.edu.au/6171, February 2014 (paginated 1–21 in repository version).

—(2012), 'Negotiating cultural identity through the arts: Fitting in third space and cultural memory', *Journal of Arts & Communities*, 3(1): 89–104. doi:10.1386/jaac.3.1.89. Accessed via http://researchrepository. murdoch.edu.au/6168, February 2014 (paginated differently in repository version).

Waller, M. A. (2001), 'Resilience in ecosystemic context: Evolution of the concept', *American Journal of Orthopsychiatry*, 71(3): 290–7.

Ward, C. (2008), 'Thinking outside the Berry boxes: New perspectives on identity, acculturation and intercultural relations', *International Journal of Intercultural Relations*, 32: 105–14.

Ward, C. A., Bochner, S. and Furnham, A. (2001), *The Psychology of Culture Shock*, London: Routledge.

Watters, C. and Ingleby, D. (2004), 'Locations of care: Meeting the mental health and social care needs of refugees in Europe', *International Journal Of Law And Psychiatry*, 27(6): 549–70.

Westerling, M. and Karvinen-Niinikoski, S. (2010), 'Theatre enriching social work with immigrants—the case of a Finnish multicultural theatre group', *European Journal of Social Work*, 13(2): 261–70.

Wilding, R. (2012), 'Mediating culture in transnational spaces: An example of young people from refugee backgrounds', *Continuum*, 26(3): 37–41.

Winston, J. (2013), 'Drama and beauty: Promise, pleasure and pedagogy', in M. Anderson and J. Dunn (eds), *How Drama Activates Learning: Contemporary Research and Practice*, London and New York: Bloomsbury, pp. 135–44.

Woodland, S. and Lachowicz, R. (2013), 'Drama and citizenship education: Tensions of creativity, content and cash', in M. Balfour (ed.), *Refugee Performance: Practical Encounters*, Bristol: Intellect, pp. 279–96.

Yaman Ntelioglou, B. (2011), '"But why do I have to take this class?" The mandatory drama-ESL class and multiliteracies pedagogy', *Research in Drama Education: The Journal of Applied Theatre and Performance, 16*(4): 595–615.

Yohani, S. C. (2008), 'Creating an ecology of hope: Arts-based interventions with refugee children', *Child and Adolescent Social Work Journal, 25*(4): 309–23.

Zuber-Skerritt, O. (2009), *Action Learning and Action Research: Songlines through Interviews*, Rotterdam: Sense Publishers.

Index

UNIVERSITY OF WINCHESTER
LIBRARY